# So You Want To Read Music....

### Margaret Veal

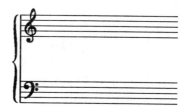

## Wren Press, Kingston-upon-Thames

## 1992

First published in 1992 by
Wren Press, Kingston-upon-Thames
8 Kelvedon Close, Kingston-upon-Thames, Surrey KT2 5LG

ISBN    0 9519914 0 X   So You Want To Read Music.... (spiral bound).

Computer-set by Trevor Dixon
196 Joel Street, Eastcote Pinner, Middlesex HA5 2PF

Laser output by Peter McBrien & Richard Owens
14 Malcolm Road, Wimbledon, London SW19 4AS

Printed in Great Britain by
Tag Instantprint, Kingston-upon-Thames, Surrey KT2 6QW

Cover design by Christine Williams

# Contents

# Acknowledgements

I would like to thank Richard for constant support and assistance,
Trevor for deciphering my appalling handwriting;
and Angela and Joanne for encouragement;

# The Alphabet of Music

With some languages such as French or Italian we share a common alphabet. Because of this, our study of that language can begin with words. In Greek or Russian, for example, the study of the language has to begin with the alphabet - that is, with the system of signs used to denote the various sounds.

Music is a language and, just like any other language, the signs or alphabet have to be learnt. It is a very straightforward and logical language, provided that you understand each step before you move on to the next.

Many people refer to learning this alphabet as "doing rudiments of music" and immediately surround it with mystique. This is a great shame. It is logical and precise. It works in the same way as any other language, in that individual letters are grouped to make words, and words are grouped into sentences and paragraphs in order to express complete thoughts. Even ten minutes work every day for a few weeks would enable you to learn this alphabet and would also enable you to begin to piece musical words together.

Having mastered the alphabet, this knowledge can be applied to every piece of music which you see. As with learning any language, the more you apply your knowledge, the more of the language of music you will be able to translate.

# Musical signs & symbols

Music is the language of sound, so the first word which has to be understood is **Pitch**. This word describes how high or how low a sound is. The pitch of every sound is written by using notes. They look like this:

People ask why it is necessary to use different sorts of notes. This is because every sound is made up of two elements:

       1 - How high or how low the note is **(pitch)**

       2 - For how long that particular note is sounded **(length)**

The length of notes will be discussed on page 5.

## Pitch

The starting point for the alphabet of music is a note found in the centre of the piano, called **Middle C**, so called because it is approximately in the *middle* of the range of sounds to which the human ear is accustomed. The notes *above* middle C become progressively higher in pitch and the notes *below* middle C become progressively lower.

A look at any piece of music will confirm that notes are written on sets of five lines and four spaces. Each set of lines and spaces is called a **staff** or **stave,** and looks like this:

One stave only gives room for nine notes to be indicated. This is only a fraction of the notes which the human ear is able to hear and which are constantly used in music. Two or more staves are often used simultaneously, so signs are needed to indicate whether the notes on a particular stave are of high or low pitch. These signs are called **clefs**.

The word **clef** needs some explanation. It is spelt **clef** in both French and English; in German it is spelt **Schlussel** and in Italian **chiave**. In all four languages the meaning is the same - KEY. That is, *key* in the sense of unlocking something. The French also has an alternative meaning: *clue*. In other words, it is the *key, clue* or *sign* to whether the pitch is *high* or *low*.

A stave without a clef has no meaning. A thousand notes can be written upon it, but no-one will know the names of those notes until a clef is inserted in order to indicate the pitch of the notes.

The sign that is used to indicate the notes *above* middle C is called a **Treble Clef**; the sign for the notes *below* middle C is called a **Bass Clef**.

**The Treble Clef** is also known as the **G clef**, because it curls around the second line of the stave and this indicates the note **G** in the treble clef. It looks like this:

**The Bass Clef** is also known as the **F clef**, because it curls around the fourth line of the stave and this indicates the note **F** in the bass clef. It looks like this:

When sitting at a piano, the bass clef notes are to the *left* of middle C and the treble clef notes are to the *right* of it. The further to the left, the deeper in pitch the notes become; the further to the right of middle C, the higher in pitch they become. The concept of pitch applies to the notes when written on the stave: the higher they are on the stave, the higher they are in pitch; the lower on the stave, the lower they are in pitch.

Every note has a name. In music, only the first seven letters of the alphabet are used:

A B C D E F G

When **G** is reached, the next note is called **A**, and so on. The distance from one letter name to where it occurs again, whether higher or lower, is eight notes, and is called an **Octave**.

A B C D E F G A B C D E F G A

one octave lower    A    one octave higher

This is a picture of three octaves on a piano keyboard, starting and finishing on C. (This is also reproduced on the flap inside the front cover.) Below it are two staves, on which are written the corresponding notes. (Observe the change of clef at middle C.)

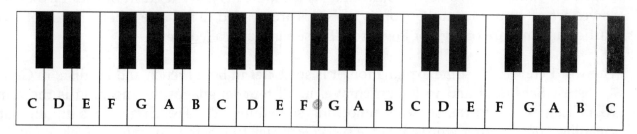

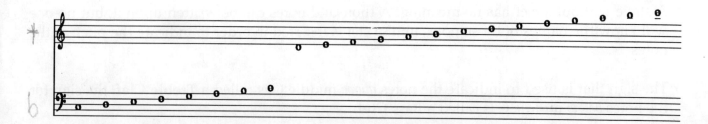

These two illustrations will need to be frequently referred to in subsequent chapters.

# The names of the lines & spaces

There is no short-cut to learning the names of the lines and spaces and little can be achieved until this is done. A huge effort at this stage will be amply repaid, because it will enable any student to move on to more interesting work, and is probably the only thing which has to be immediately memorised. Any short-cuts are guaranteed to result in later problems!

The letters follow each other strictly alphabetically. A note on a line is followed by one on a space. For example, if **E** is on a line, then **F** will be in space above. From line to line, or from space to space, a letter name - and therefore a note - is skipped. It follows that, if **E** is on a line, **G** will be on the line above and **F** in the space in between. The easiest way to memorize the names of the notes is to group separately the lines and the spaces.

**Note carefully:**
As notes go *up* the stave, they go *forwards* through the alphabet and become *higher* in pitch. As notes go *down* the stave, they go *backwards* through the alphabet and become *lower* in pitch.

**The notes of the Treble Clef** (*above* middle C):

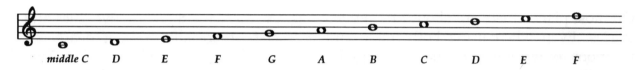

The lines of the treble clef are **E G B D F**, which can easily be remembered by the mnemonic

**E  G  B  D  F**
Every Good Boy Deserves Food

The spaces of the treble clef are **F A C E**, easily remembered because of the word they spell.

**The notes of the Bass Clef** (*below* middle C):

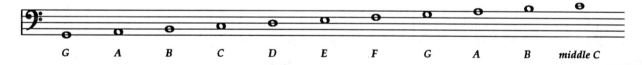

The lines of the bass clef are **G B D F A**:

**G  B  D  F  A**
Good Boys Deserve Food Always

The spaces of the bass clef are **A C E G**:

**A  C  E  G**
All Cows Eat Grass

A useful exercise to reinforce the memorisation of these notes is to make up words using the first seven letters of the alphabet and then to write them onto the stave as notes using both the bass and treble clefs. A variety of words can be made, for example: CAB, DEAF, BADGE, CABBAGE, FACADE.

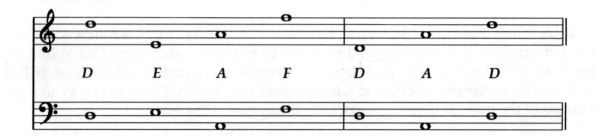

The more these signs are used, the more quickly they will be memorised.

# Ledger Lines

On most pianos there are about fifty white notes. On the stave there are five lines and four spaces. Even when using both treble and bass clefs, there still are not nearly enough positions for writing all the notes. The problem is solved by the use of ledger lines. These are small lines just large enough for one note placed above or below the stave. In fact, middle C is written on a ledger line. Just as a space is created between any two lines on the stave, so a space is created between two ledger lines, or between the ledger line immediately above or below the stave.

For the notes above F on the top line in the treble clef, ledger lines are used as follows:

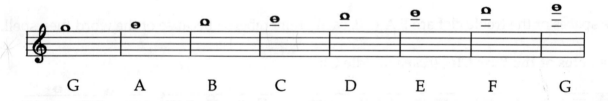

This also illustrates the use of the spaces between the ledger lines.

For the notes below G on the first line of the bass clef, ledger lines are used as follows:

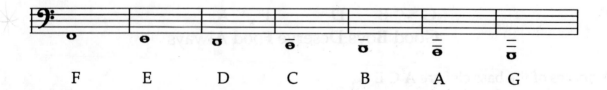

# The lengths of notes & rests

Every piece of music has its own *pulse* or *beat*. This is the quality that sets hands clapping and toes tapping and is responsible for injecting life into the music. The pulse, as with human beings, is the sign of life which throbs, maybe at different speeds, for the entire life of that body.

A **note** can be thought of as representing a sound and a **rest** as representing a silence. A system is therefore needed to indicate how long each note or rest should be. A different symbol is used according to the length of each note or rest. In the table below, the symbol for each note and its equivalent rest is given, together with its European and American name. **It will be seen that each subsequent note is an exact fraction of the semibreve.**

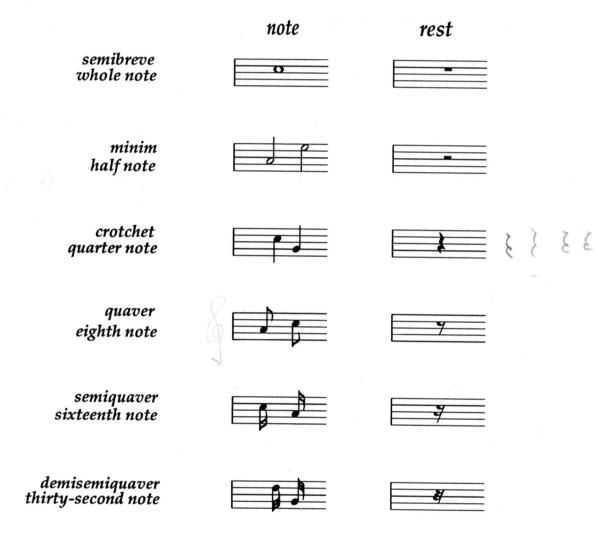

## The Breve

There is a note which is twice as long as a semibreve. It is called a **breve**. The note is shown in example *A* and the rest in example *B*:

    A                    B

Breves are most frequently used in hymn tunes.

## Dotted notes & rests

A dot *at the side of* a note or a rest lengthens the note or rest by half its value.

A minim plus a crotchet equals a dotted minim    ♩ + ♩ = ♩.

A crotchet rest plus a quaver rest equals a dotted crotchet rest    𝄽 + 𝄾 = 𝄽.

## Double-dotted notes & rests

If a composer adds two dots to a note or rest, the first dot, as already explained, takes half the value of the *note*; the second dot will take half the value of the *first* dot. For example,

A double-dotted minim equals a minim plus a crotchet plus a quaver  ♩.. = ♩ + ♩ + ♪

A double-dotted crotchet rest equals a crotchet plus a quaver plus a semi-quaver.

♩.. = ♩ + ♪ + ♬

## The slur

A slur is the sign used when two or more notes of *different* pitch need to be joined together smoothly:

When a slur is used to join the notes of an entire phrase, it is often referred to as a **phrase mark**.

## Tied notes

When two notes of the same letter name and at the *same* pitch are joined by a curve, the second note is not sounded, but adds its value to the first note. In this instance, the curve is called a **tie**.

# Time Signatures

## Bars & bar-lines

A **bar** is a slice, or fraction, of music, just like a slice or part of a cake. **Bar-lines** are vertical lines through the stave dividing the music up into bars.

At the end of each section or piece of music, two bar-lines are drawn close together:

## Accents

In speech, some syllables are more heavily stressed than others. For example, the following line

*If music be the food of love, play on*

can be stressed:

If **MU**sic be the **FOOD** of love, play **ON**.

The stressed, or accented, syllables are in large type, the unaccented syllables are small. To stress it in any other way would sound very odd, because words have natural accents. In the same way, music has natural accents, and the strongest accent always occurs immediately after the bar-line, thereby falling on the first beat of the bar. If a composer wants to give a different note importance, an **accent** sign > is used. This instructs the performer to make that particular note stand out, usually - but not always - by making it louder.

## Understanding time-signatures

As discussed on page 5, all music has a pulse or beat. The fraction at the beginning of a piece of music is called the **time signature**. It gives the *number* of beats in every bar and the *type of note* which is the beat. Most music consists of 2 or 3 beats in a bar, or multiples of 2 or 3. It seems natural to march to music which has 2, or a multiple of 2, beats in a bar; it seems natural to waltz to music which has 3 beats in a bar.

There are two sorts of time in music: **simple** and **compound**.

In **Simple Time**, the beat is an ordinary note - a minim ♩ or a crotchet ♩ or a quaver ♪ - and it can be divided into two.

In **Compound Time**, the beat is a dotted note - a dotted minim ♩. or a dotted crotchet ♩.

or a dotted quaver ♪. - and it can be divided into three.

# Simple Time

In simple time, the top figure of the time signature states the number of beats in the bar. The bottom figure states what *type* of note the *beat* is, that is, whether the beat is a minim, a crochet or a quaver. For example, in the time signature $^2_4$

    **2**       means that there are two beats in a bar
    **4**       means that the beat is a crochet, or quarter note
(This illustrates why a knowledge of the American time names of notes is so helpful: see page 5.)

Similarly:
    **3**       means that there are three beats in every bar
    **2**       means that the beat is a minim, or half note

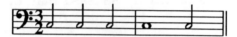

    **4**       means that there are four beats in every bar
    **8**       means that the beat is a quaver, or eighth note

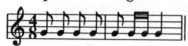

From these illustrations it can be seen that the time signature of $^4_4$ means that there are four crotchet beats in every bar.

Another way of writing this time signature is by using the symbol  **C**  placed on the stave where the time signature would normally be written. When this symbol is used, the music is often said to be in **common time**.

In the same way, the time signature of $^2_2$ means that there are two minim beats in every bar.

This is often shown by the symbol  **¢**  When this symbol is used the music is generally said to be in **split time**.

The beats provide the *skeleton* or *framework* of the bar, but individual notes or rests can be of a longer or shorter duration than one beat.

# Grouping of notes & rests

If notes are written separately, it is sometimes extremely difficult for the eye to work out how they should be played. In example A, the notes are written individually; in example B the notes are of exactly the same length, but because they are grouped together - each group totalling one beat - it is much easier for the eye to distinguish them.

*Example A*                                                        *Example B*

The rule for the grouping of notes is very simple. They are generally grouped so that they add up to one beat.

There are four exceptions to this general rule:

1        In $\frac{2}{4}$ time, if a whole bar consists of quavers, these four quavers should be grouped together.

2        In $\frac{4}{4}$ time, if either the *first* half of the bar or the *second* half of the bar consists of four quavers, these should be grouped together. It is *completely wrong* to join together the *second* and *third* beats.

*correct*                                        *incorrect*

3        In $\frac{3}{4}$ or $\frac{3}{8}$ time, if a bar consists only of quavers, these should be grouped together.

4        In $\frac{3}{8}$ time, if a bar consists of six semiquavers, these should be grouped together.

If a group contains a semiquaver in music where the beat is a crotchet, the notes should be grouped into single beats.

*acceptable    better*

# Where a tune begins

Many tunes begin on the first beat of the bar, but not *all* music begins that way. In fact, a tune may begin on *any* part of the bar or even part way through a beat. It is possible to begin half way through a bar, as in example A, or on the last beat of the bar, as in examples B and C. A tune may even begin in the middle of a *beat*. Example D begins on the final quaver of a bar, which in $^2_4$ time is only worth half a beat.

*Example A*                                             *Example B*

*Example C*                                             *Example D*

Where a tune begins is entirely up to the composer. However the first and last bars *must* total a complete bar of music in the given time signature. This can be more easily seen by looking at the following examples:

# Grouping of rests

The grouping of rests follows the same principle as the grouping of notes, that is, a separate rest should be used for every beat (*Examples A and B, below*). Where there are four beats in a bar, the same rule applies for rests as for notes, that is, a single rest may be used for the *first* or *second* half of the bar (*Examples C and E, below*), but not for the *middle* of the bar covering the second and third beats (*Example D, below*).

*Examples:*   A                B                    C                D                E

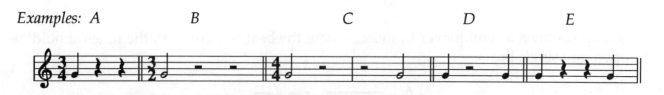

In examinations, candidates are often asked to insert the appropriate rests into a bar which contains notes. If the first note is not *a complete beat*, add a rest - or rests - to complete that beat. The remainder of the bar should be completed as follows:

1      If the time signature indicates 2 or 3 beats in the bar, add rests to make *separate whole beats*. *(Example F)*

2      If the time signature indicates 4 beats in the bar, complete the half bar, and finally use a rest of two beats in value to complete the second half of the bar. *(Example G)*

3      If there are notes in the second half of the bar, these must be dealt with in the same way as the first half of the bar. *(Example H)*

*Example F*      *Example G*      *Example H*

Where a composer wishes to indicate a complete bar's rest or silence, the semibreve rest is used in all time signatures, except that of $^4_2$ - regardless of whether the music is in simple or compound time. In $^4_2$ time a *breve* rest is used to indicate a complete bar's silence.

# Triplets

In simple time, the beat is an ordinary note - that is, a minim, a crotchet or a quaver - which divides naturally into two. For example, a minim equals two crotchets, a crotchet equals two quavers, and so on. Sometimes a composer needs the beat to be divided into *three* equal notes. This is known as a **triplet** and is indicated by a group of three equal notes joined by a slur with a figure 3.

# Writing a reply to a given rhythm

An understanding of rhythm and of the effect it produces is essential in order to understand music. From even the earliest grades, examination boards will look for this understanding. The importance of rhythm, pulse or beat and the varying lengths of notes has already been stated, so it is logical to harness this information by developing the skill of inventing rhythms. The first stage is to be able to add a balanced answer to a given rhythmic phrase. Because the pitch of the note is not involved, the rhythm should be written on one note only and a clef or a key signature is not needed. Where notes vary in pitch, they form a melody and the process of writing a melody will be studied at a later stage. Think of a rhythm as something which can be tapped out on a percussion instrument, for example a drum or a castanet, or on one note of a piano. It is correct to write it on one note of the stave, or even to write the notes without a line.

This is really the first stage in composition, but, even here, the following essentials must be apparent:

## 1 Accuracy
The total value of the notes and rests in every bar must equal the time signature. The correctly-grouped notes and rests are the basic minimum. The rhythm must also make *musical* sense. Example A is mathematically correct, but the effect is just that of a jumble of notes. Compare it with example B.

Example A                              Example B

Make every effort to *hear* the rhythm. Begin by setting a steady tempo and a firm beat, then tap out the beats for two or four bars, stressing the first beat of the bar. Gradually a musical shape will begin to emerge.

## 2 Balance
The reply must balance the original statement, thereby giving a sense of completeness. In order to achieve this, it is necessary to *feel* the opening statement. Again there is no substitute for tapping out the beats and then tapping out the actual rhythm of the statement.

## 3 Imagination
Musical imagination must be evident or the rhythm will be completely mechanical and unmusical. This is the ingredient which lifts ordinary work into a different class, but it is also the most difficult to describe. In example C every note is of the same length and is therefore rather boring. In example D the notes are of varying lengths, giving the rhythm much greater interest.

Example C                              Example D

There is no blueprint for writing an interesting rhythm, melody, or even a letter. The interest is supplied by the imagination of the writer and every writer would produce something different. However, here are some basic guidelines:

1)      Always keep in mind the chosen steady tempo and steady beat.

2)      Do not simply repeat what has already been stated. It will not show any understanding of the question or give any indication of musical imagination.

3)      On the other hand, a distinctive feature of the given rhythm may be used, perhaps in a different place in the bar, or even turned around.

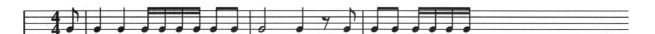

4)      A rhythm can begin on any part of the bar. When it does not start at the beginning of the bar, the first and last bars must total a complete bar.

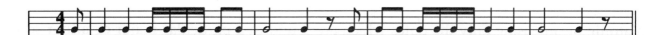

5)      The last note of the rhythm needs to produce a feeling of finality. This is more easily achieved by using a note equal in length to at least one beat. Frequently a longer note than that is effective.

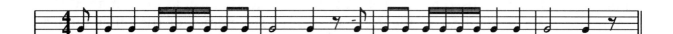

# Scales

A scale is a ladder of sounds, derived from the Italian *scala*, meaning *ladder, steps* or *stairs*.

Scales originated for a number of reasons. These may include intuition, instinct, reasoning, coincidence, or any combination of these. Some very early scales are built in such a way that science shows that they agree with mathematical - and therefore acoustical - principles. Scientists such as Pythagoras conducted practical experiments and the theoretical results of these continue to affect our knowledge of scales.

Perhaps the true origin of scales is connected with speech and its various inflections. We expect a person from Manchester to speak differently from a person from Cornwall, Scotland or Wales. The differences lie in the way the pitch of the voice varies and the differing stresses on individual words or syllables. If people from the same country vary in the way in which they speak, those from different countries can certainly be expected to have different speech patterns and it follows that some of these variations will be audible in their music.

Some scales are more familiar than others to Western ears, but it should not be automatically assumed that this makes them more important. It is simpler to start by looking at the most easily recognisable scales, namely those most frequently heard. They are known as **diatonic scales**.

**Diatonic** means using only the notes which are found in a particular **major** or **minor** scale. The *everyday* meaning of the word **major** is *greater* and of **minor** is *lesser*. This is also an acceptable *musical* meaning.

Major and minor scales appear to have evolved very slowly from earlier **modes**. Modes were the types of scales on which ecclesiastical plainsong was built. Each mode had a Greek name, although these are rarely used today. The C major scale is identical to the **Ionian Mode** and the A minor scale is identical to the **Aeolian Mode**. The names of the other modes are: **Dorian, Phrygian, Lydian** and **Mixolydian**.

## Tones and semitones

A **semitone** is the distance from one note to its nearest neighbour.
A **tone** equals two semitones.

In any tune, every note has to be the right distance from the previous note. Most people can sing up a scale, which is really a simple tune, but only rarely does a scale consist entirely of semitones. When it does it is called a **chromatic scale**. This will be discussed on page 46. The scale which most people automatically think of is known in musical terms as a **major scale** and this consists of a precise order of tones and semitones.

To produce a **major scale**, the distances between the notes occur in the following order:

From the *first* to the *second* note, the distance is                    **a tone.**
From the *second* to the *third* note, the distance is                     **a tone.**
From the *third* to the *fourth* note, the distance is                     **a semitone.**
From the *fourth* to the *fifth* note, the distance is                     a **tone.**
From the *fifth* to the *sixth* note, the distance is                      a **tone.**
From the *sixth* to the *seventh* note, the distance is                    a **tone.**
From the *seventh* to the *eighth* note, the distance is                   **a semitone.**

## Scale of C major

This is the normal starting point for understanding the construction of a major scale. Because it uses only the white notes of the keyboard, it is unnecessary to alter any note in order to make the correct pattern of tones and semitones.

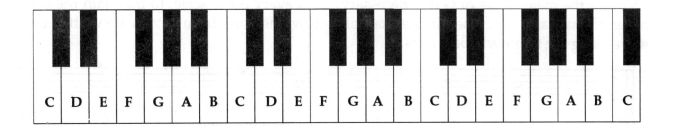

Frequent reference to the illustration of a keyboard above or inside the front cover will make the working-out of scales a simple process.

The notes which comprise the scale of C are: **C D E F G A B C**   This makes one octave. Keeping in mind that a semitone is the distance from one note to its nearest neighbour and that a tone equals two semitones, the keyboard can be used to check the distance between each pair of notes.

From **C** to **D** is        **a tone**        (because there is a black note between them)
From **D** to **E** is        **a tone**        (because there is a black note between them)
From **E** to **F** is        **a semitone**    (because there is *no* black note between them)
From **F** to **G** is        **a tone**        (because there is a black note between them)
From **G** to **A** is        **a tone**        (because there is a black note between them)
From **A** to **B** is        **a tone**        (because there is a black note between them)
From **B** to **C** is        **a semitone**    (because there is *no* black note between them)

**This order of tones and semitones has to be maintained in order to produce every major scale.**

The example below gives this scale written on the stave using treble and bass clefs respectively. Notice that the notes are identical whether the scale is ascending or descending.

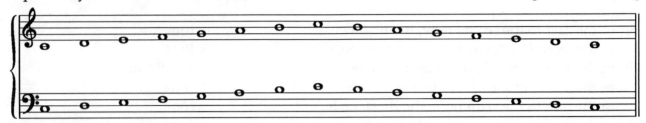

The scale falls naturally into two groups of four notes. Each group is called a **tetrachord**. This word comes from the Greek language: *tetra*, meaning four; *chorde*, meaning note or string.

## Scale of G major

The octave from G to G contains the following letter-names: **G A B C D E F G**
To build the major scale of G it is necessary, as in every other scale, to maintain the correct order of tones and semitones. In the example below, the notes from G to G are written on the stave using the treble and bass clefs.

By comparing each pair of notes with the keyboard it can be seen that the order of tones and semitones is maintained until F. At that point F needs to be a tone away from E, but it is only a semitone. By raising F a semitone it is moved to the nearest black note. Obviously a sign is needed to give this instruction. This sign is called a **sharp**, and looks like this:

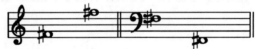

The important part of the sharp sign is the box in the middle. This *must* go precisely in the space, or around the line, which the note is on.

The correct version of the scale of G is:

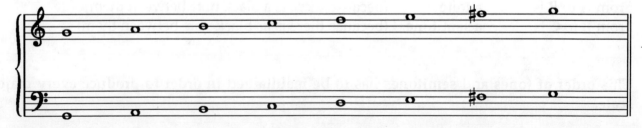

The *second* tetrachord of the C major scale forms the *first* tetrachord of the G major scale.

## Scale of D major

In this scale *two* notes - F and C - need to be sharpened so as to keep the correct order of tones and semitones,. The scale, correctly written, is:

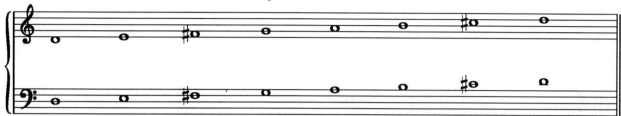

The *second* tetrachord of the G major scale forms the *first* tetrachord of the D major scale. **This pattern continues throughout the major scales which contain sharps.**

## Scale of A major

Here, *three* notes need to be sharpened: F, C and G.

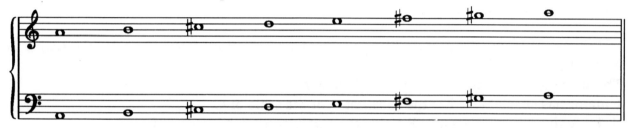

The starting point was the scale of C major.
**G major** has *one* sharp and G is the *fifth* note of the scale of C.
**D major** has *two* sharps and D is the *fifth* note of the scale of G.
**A major** has *three* sharps and A is the *fifth* note of the scale of D.
This pattern is constant throughout the scales which contain sharps.

## Scale of F major

In some scales it is necessary not to *raise* notes, but to *lower* them so as to maintain the correct order of tones and semitones.
The octave from F to F contains the following letter-names:  **F  G  A  B  C  D  E  F**  In the examples below, these notes are written on the stave using the treble and bass clefs.

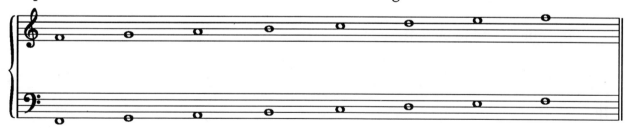

By using the keyboard and the same process as before, it is apparent that the order of tones and semitones is not maintained between **A** and **B**. At that point, a *semitone* is needed, but B is a *tone* away from A. By lowering B to the black note below, the correct order is maintained.

The sign for this is called a **flat** and looks like this:

As with the sharp sign, the important part of the flat is the part which goes precisely around the line or space.

The correct scale of F major looks like this:

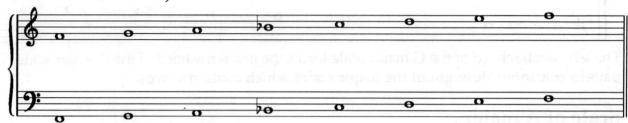

By comparing this example with the scale of C major, it can be seen that the *first* tetrachord of C major forms the *second* tetrachord of F major. **This pattern is maintained throughout all scales which contain flats.**

In the same way as the *sharp* scales follow each other *five notes higher*, the *flat* scales follow each other *four notes higher*.
The starting point is again the scale of C major.
**F major** has *one* flat and **F** is the *fourth* note of the scale of **C**.
**B flat major** has *two* flats and **B flat** is the *fourth* note of the scale of **F**.
**E flat major** has *three* flats and **E flat** is the *fourth* note of the scale of **B flat**.

## Scale of B flat major

To keep the correct order of tones and semitones, *two* notes need to be flattened in this scale.

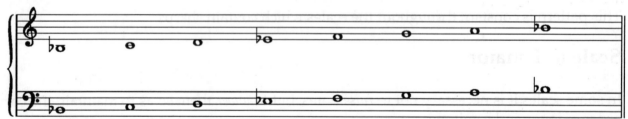

## Scale of E flat major

Here, *three* notes need to be flattened.

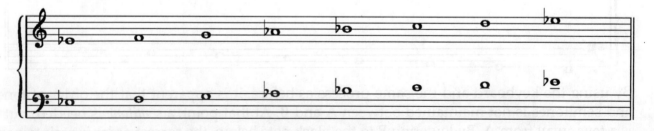

# Accidentals

A **sharp** *raises* a note by a semitone; a **flat** *lowers* a note by a semitone. If a composer needs to cancel either of these, a sign called a **natural** is used. It looks like this:

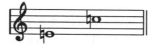

As with the sharp sign, it is the box in the middle which has to be placed precisely around the same line or in the same space as the note to which it applies.

Sharps, flats and naturals are all called **accidentals** and all are placed *before* the note to which they apply. All accidentals last only to the end of the bar in which they are written but apply to *every* note of the same letter-name and *at the same pitch* in that bar, no matter how many times that note is repeated.

Occasionally it is necessary to raise or lower a note by *two* semitones, ie. by a tone. The sign for this is a double sharp shown as ✗ and the sign for a double flat is shown as ♭♭ To cancel either of these signs and so to revert to an *ordinary* sharpened or flattened note, the *original* sharp or flat sign is used.

In earlier music, the cancellation of a sharp or flat was shown as follows:

♮ ♯ 𝅝                    ♮ ♭ 𝅝

# Key Signatures

Instead of writing accidentals before every note, they can be put together at the beginning of every line. This saves a great deal of writing. These sharps or flats, when they are grouped together in this way, are called the **key signature** and immediately indicate what scale is being used and therefore what key the music is in. Unlike the use of accidentals, which only apply to individual notes in the bar in which they appear, sharps and flats used in the key signature apply to *every* note of that letter-name *at every pitch*.

The key signatures of the following scales look like this; they are given for both the treble and bass clefs.

G Major          D Major          A Major

F                C F              C F G

F Major  Bb Major  Eb Major

It can be seen that the sharps and flats occur in a very precise order, and the key signature is incorrect if that order is not maintained. The reason for this is musical. C major has no sharps or flats. G major has one sharp - *F sharp*.

When moving to the scale with two sharps, the existing sharp (*F sharp*) is automatically carried forward and will always appear first in the key signature. So the scale with two sharps will have a key signature beginning with F sharp and then one other note - *C sharp*. The scale with three sharps will have a key signature beginning with F sharp, C sharp and then one other note - *G sharp*.

This same principle applies to the scales which contain flats.

It is both unnecessary and incorrect to use a key signature and then, later in the scale, to write accidentals before the notes which the key signature has already altered. For example, in the key of G major it is wrong to put a sharp before the note F if the key signature has already been written in. In examinations, the question will usually state whether a key signature or accidentals is required.

# Triads

A **triad** is a chord consisting of three notes. The middle note is the distance of a third away from the lowest note and the top note is a third away from the middle note. To find this distance, simply omit a letter name. For example:

**E** is a third away from **C**, D having been omitted.
**G** is a third away from **E**, F having been omitted.

The triad on **C** will consist of **C   E   G**   (D and F having been omitted).
The triad on **G** will consist of **G   B   D**   (A and C having been omitted).
The triad on **F** will consist of  **F   A   C**    (G and B flat having been omitted).

It can be seen from this that a triad formed on the first note of the scale uses the *first, third* and *fifth* notes of that scale. The correct musical name for the first note of a scale is the **tonic** (from *tone note* or *key note*). Therefore a triad formed on the first note or *tonic* of the scale is known as a **tonic triad**.

> The bottom note of the triad is called the **root**.
> The middle note of the triad is called the **third**.
> The top note of the triad is called the **fifth**.

Any of the three notes of the triad can be the lowest note.

> When the root is the lowest note, the triad is in **root position**.
> When the third is the lowest note, the triad is in its **first inversion**.
> When the fifth is the lowest note, the triad is in its **second inversion**.

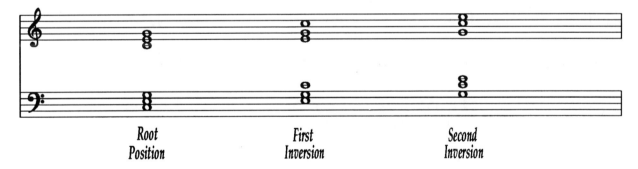

Root
Position

First
Inversion

Second
Inversion

From this example, it can be seen that:

When the lowest note of the triad is the root (**C**), the middle note is the third (**E**) and the top note the fifth (**G**).
When the lowest note of the triad is the third (**E**), the middle note is the fifth (**G**) and the top note is the root (**C**).
When the lowest note of the triad is the fifth (**G**), the middle note is the root (**C**) and the top note is the third (**E**).

# Compound time

In compound time, the beat is divisible by three. This means:

A ♩. beat divides into ♩♩♩      A ♩. beat divides into ♪♪♪

A ♪. beat divides into ♪♪♪

## Time signatures in compound time

When the top figure of the time signature is 6, 9 or 12, the time is **compound**. To find the number of beats in a bar this top figure of 6, 9 or 12 must be divided by three.
It follows, then that    6   means   2   beats in a bar,
                    9   means   3   beats in a bar and
            12   means   4   beats in a bar.

To find the note which constitutes one beat, it is necessary to learn the following:

When the lower figure of the time signature is 4, the beat will be a dotted minim ♩.

When the lower figure of the time signature is 8, the beat will be a dotted crotchet ♩.

When the lower figure of the time signature is 16, the beat will be a dotted quaver ♪.

Because the top figure of the time signature can only be 6, 9 or 12, thereby indicating two, three or four beats in a bar, compound time is easily recognised.
To illustrate this:

$^6_4$ indicates two dotted minim beats in every bar

$^9_4$ indicates three dotted minim beats in every bar

$^{12}_4$ indicates four dotted minim beats in every bar
(Note: this time signature is hardly ever used.)

$^6_8$ indicates two dotted crotchet beats in every bar

$^9_8$ indicates three dotted crotchet beats in every bar

$^{12}_8$ indicates four dotted crotchet beats in every bar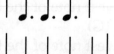

**6₁₆** indicates two dotted quaver beats in every bar

**9₁₆** indicates three dotted quaver beats in every bar

**12₁₆** indicates four dotted quaver beats in every bar

By using the American time names, the content of each bar can be seen exactly. However, this method does not give the number of *beats*, but the number of *notes*, in every bar. This is an important difference between compound and simple time. For example, using the American time names, the time signature of **6₈** indicates that there are six eighth notes, or quavers, in every bar; it does *not* indicate six *beats* in a bar. As stated earlier, the top figure of **6**, whilst immediately indicating compound time, also indicates that the number of beats in a bar is **2**, each being a dotted crotchet.

## Grouping of notes & rests in compound time

In compound time it is absolutely essential to make the divisions of the beats really clear because in some time signatures confusion could occur between simple and compound time if this is not done. For example, the time signatures of **6₈** and **3₄** might be confused if the grouping is blurred because they both contain six quavers in every bar.

A comparison of these two examples shows that where the notes are of the same length the correct grouping is crucial in order to distinguish one time signature from another.

Regardless of whether the beat is a dotted minim, a dotted crotchet or a dotted quaver, the same rule must be applied. Notes *must* be grouped to make up *one* beat.

A rest lasting for one beat can be indicated either by two rests, or by a dotted rest. Both are correct.

♩. may be shown by ⁊ · or by ⁊ ⁊

The rules for completing with rests a bar that already contains some notes is exactly the same as for simple time. First complete the beat and then use a rest for each subsequent beat. When there are four beats in a bar, a single rest may be used for the first or second half of the bar but a single rest may not be used to cover the second and third beats. When completing a beat do not use one rest of longer value than the given note. For example:

**6₈**     ♪⁊⁊ ⁊⁊  is correct          **6₈**     ♪⁊ ⁊⁊  is incorrect

# Duplets

Sometimes a dotted note needs to be divided into two. This is called a **duplet** and is usuall[y]
shown by a figure 2 above the notes. For example:

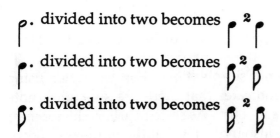

People with sharp eyes and mathematical brains will say that *two* crotchets do not equal [a]
dotted minim; a dotted minim equals *three* crotchets. Normally this is so, but it is the duple[t]
which makes the difference and that difference is reflected in the sound. When two crotchet[s]
have a duplet over them it means that it is a dotted minim, not an ordinary minim which i[s]
being divided by two. In effect:

Some composers do not use the duplet sign; they merely write it out as it sounds. Becaus[e]
the duplet is used to divide a dotted note, it is used more in compound time where the bea[t]
is a dotted note than in simple time where it is *not*.

# Duple, triple and quadruple time

Music with **two** beats in a bar is said to be in **duple** time.
Music with **three** beats in a bar is said to be in **triple** time.
Music with **four** beats in a bar is said to be in **quadruple** time.

Two beats in a bar in **simple** time is called **simple duple** time.
Two beats in a bar in **compound** time is called **compound duple** time.

Three beats in a bar in **simple** time is called **simple triple** time.
Three beats in a bar in **compound** time is called **compound triple** time.

Four beats in a bar in **simple** time is called **simple quadruple** time.
Four beats in a bar in **compound** time is called **compound quadruple** time.

# The Minor Scale

The minor scale forms a tune in exactly the same way as the major scale, but because the order of tones and semitones is different, the tune is different. There are two forms of the minor scale: **harmonic** and **melodic**.

## The harmonic form

The minor scale without any sharps or flats in the key signature begins on A. **A minor** is the **relative minor** of C major because it is the minor *equivalent*. Conversely, C major is the **relative major** of A minor. The term **relative** applies to scales in both the major and minor which share the same key signature. The *first three notes* of both the harmonic and melodic minor scales are the same as the *last three notes* of their relative major scale. Therefore the minor scale begins on the sixth note of its relative major scale. The major scale begins on the third note of its relative minor scale.

The order of tones and semitones is fixed, like that of the major scale, and is as follows:

> **one tone**
> **one semitone**
> **two separate tones**
> **one semitone**
> **a large jump equal to three semitones, ie. a tone and a half**
> **one semitone**

The distance from the first to the third note in a minor scale (known as a **minor third**) is a semitone smaller than the distance from the first to the third note in a major scale (known as a **major third**). This is the most crucial factor in establishing the differing characteristics of major and minor.

*C - E MAJOR = MAJOR THIRD (A TONE APART)*
*MINOR A - C = SEMITONE APART (MINOR THIRD)*

**One important fact**
To make any scale sound acceptable to Western ears, there has to be a semitone between the seventh and the eighth notes. Therefore an adjustment has to be made in all minor scales to achieve this. Whatever form this adjustment of the seventh note takes to ensure that it is a semitone away from the eighth note, it is achieved by writing an accidental. This does not form part of the key signature, nor does it ever appear in it.

## The A minor scale

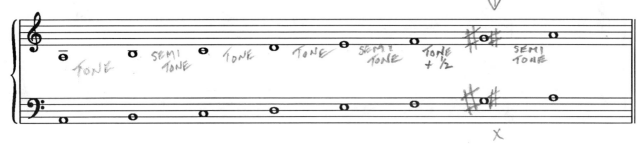

The example above shows one octave of a scale starting on A. When the order of tones and semitones is worked out, it can be seen that this forms the harmonic minor scale up to and including F. The next note needs to be a distance of three semitones away, but G is only a tone, or two semitones, away from F and therefore needs to be raised by a semitone, becoming G sharp. G sharp to A is a semitone and so correctly completes the scale. *G sharp does <u>not</u> form part of the key signature or appear in it.*

Below is the correct version of **A <u>harmonic</u> minor scale**. As with the major scales, the notes are the same both ascending and descending.

On page 18 it was observed that in the major scales the sharp key signatures followed each five notes higher and the flat key signatures four notes higher. The principle is exactly the same in the minor scales. The key of A minor has no flats or sharps; its fifth note is E, and so **E minor** will contain one sharp.

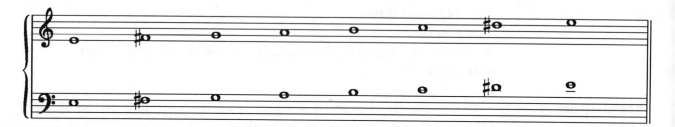

The scale of **B minor** has two sharps.

The scale of **F sharp minor** has three sharps.

The fourth note of A minor is D; the **D minor** scale will contain one flat.

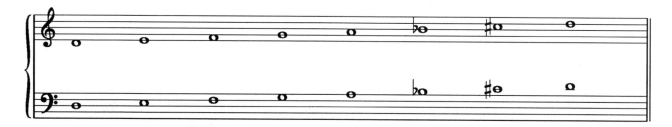

The scale of **G minor** has two flats.

The scale of **C minor** has three flats.

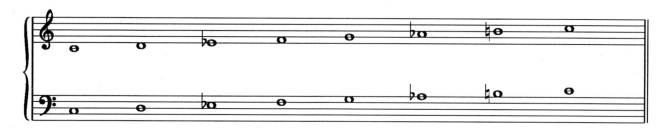

# The melodic form

Because the distance - or to use the correct word, **interval** - which occurs between the sixth and seventh notes in the harmonic minor scale is large and awkward, another version of the minor scale has evolved, namely the **melodic minor**. Melodic is an apt description of it. By eliminating this awkward interval, the scale is much easier to sing. In effect, it is more of a *melody*. To keep the melodic qualities, the scale is different descending from ascending. This arose because some composers - largely in the eighteenth century - discovered that it was more agreeable and satisfying melodically if the sixth and seventh notes were sharpened when ascending, but that these notes were not altered when descending. In other words, when descending the notes are *exactly* those of the key signature.

In both forms of the minor scale, any alterations to the sixth or the seventh notes are *never* shown in the key signature.
In the melodic minor scale, the sixth and seventh notes are altered only when ascending, these alterations being cancelled when descending.
In the harmonic form only the seventh note is altered, both when ascending and descending.

**Page 27**

When the melodic minor scale is *ascending*, the distances are:
> **one tone**
> **one semitone**
> **four separate tones**
> **one semitone**

When the melodic minor scale is *descending*, the notes are exactly those of the key signature.

The first five notes of the scale are the same in both the harmonic and melodic forms. Between the fifth and the sixth notes, and the sixth and the seventh notes, there must be intervals of a tone. Between the seventh and the eighth notes, there must of necessity be an interval of a semitone in order to avoid it sounding incorrect to Western ears. It can be seen from this that when ascending, only the sixth note is different between the melodic and harmonic scales. When descending, the seventh note is different.

**A melodic minor:**

**E melodic minor:**

**B melodic minor:**

**F sharp melodic minor:**

**D melodic minor:**

**G melodic minor:**

**C melodic minor:**

# Technical names of notes or degrees of the scale

The word **degree** is really a synonym for **note**. For example, the third degree of the scale is the third note of the scale. These will be described in the order of their predominance in relation to Western hearing.

**First note**          **TONIC**

     Perhaps derived from *tone note*, meaning key or home note.

**Fifth note**          **DOMINANT**

     So called because it is next in importance to the tonic. It has a central position in harmony and melody, in both of which it certainly plays a dominating role.

**Fourth note**          **SUB-DOMINANT**

     This has nothing to do with being underneath the dominant. A better term would be *lower dominant* because it is the same distance below the tonic as the dominant is above it. It is slightly less dominating than the dominant in both harmony and melody.

**Seventh note**          **LEADING NOTE**

     This has a very important role in a great deal of Western music because it leads the ear to the tonic or key note. For this reason it must be as near to the tonic as possible, that is, a semitone away.

**Third note**          **MEDIANT**

     So called because it lies halfway between the tonic and the dominant.

**Sixth note**          **SUB-MEDIANT**

     Similarly, this lies halfway between the tonic and the *sub-dominant*.

**Second note**          **SUPER TONIC**

     This means *above* the tonic, not *superior* to it. In both major and minor scales the super tonic lies a tone above the tonic.

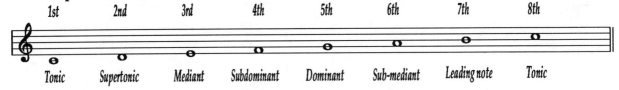

**Please note:**

When the scale is *descending*, the technical name of each note is maintained. For example, in the scale of C major, **D** is the super tonic and remains so whether ascending or descending. Similarly **B** is the leading note and remains so.

**Page 30**

# Further major scales

The major scales which begin on C, G, D, A, F, B flat and E flat were explained and written out beginning on page 15. Below, the remaining major scales are set out.

**E Major**

**B Major**

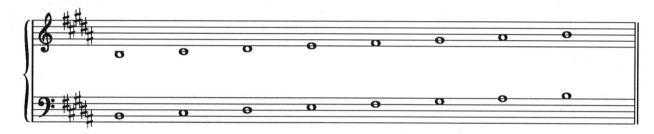

**F sharp Major**

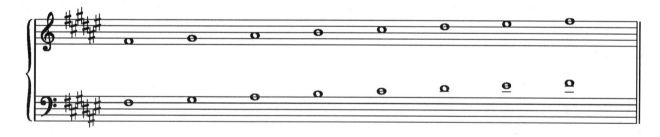

**C sharp Major**

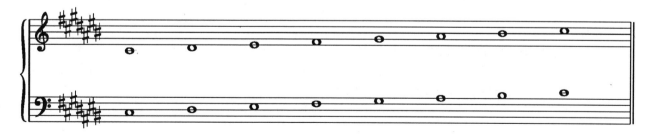

**A flat Major**

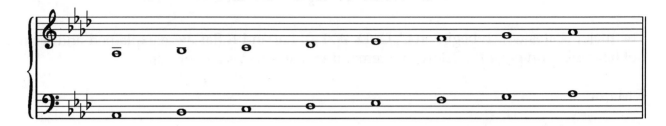

**D flat Major**   G A B D E

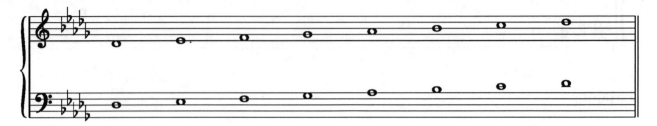

**G flat Major**

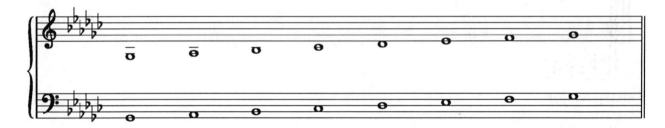

**C flat Major**

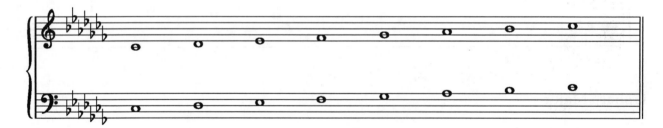

Page 32

# Simple Musical terms & definitions

Although music is a world-wide language, most musical terms are in Italian. The entire list of Italian terms is obviously extensive, but they do not need to be learnt all at once. However, the terms listed here should be learnt in order to make sense of musical notation. A fuller list is given in appendix 2. Some French and German terms are also in fairly constant use and these are also given in appendix 2.

## Dynamics

The correct name for the piano is *pianoforte*, that is an instrument which can play both softly (*piano*) and loudly (*forte*). Composers need to indicate whether music is to be loud or soft and so they use terms based on *piano* and *forte*.

| | | |
|---|---|---|
| *pianissimo* | *pp* | very quietly |
| *piano* | *p* | quietly |
| *mezzo piano* | *mp* | moderately quietly |
| *mezzo forte* | *mf* | moderately loudly |
| *forte* | *f* | loudly |
| *fortissimo* | *ff* | very loudly |
| | | |
| *crescendo* | *cresc.* | gradually getting louder |
| *diminuendo* | *dim.* | gradually getting quieter |

## Speed

| | |
|---|---|
| *lento* | very slow |
| *largo* | broad and stately |
| *adagio* | slow, leisurely |
| *andante* | at a walking pace |
| *andantino* (literally "a little andante") | two meanings: a little faster or a little slower than andante |
| *moderato* | at a moderate pace |
| *allegro* | merry, lively, fast |
| *allegretto* (literally "a little allegro") | a little slower than allegro |
| *vivace* | lively |
| *presto* | very fast |
| *prestissimo* | as fast as possible |

| | | |
|---|---|---|
| *accelerando* | *accel.* | gradually getting faster |
| *rallentando* | *rall.* | gradually getting slower |
| *ritardando* | *ritard.* | gradually getting slower |
| *ritenuto* | *rit.* | immediately slower |
| *a tempo* | | resume the normal speed |
| *allargando* | | increasing both the tone and the speed |
| *meno mosso* | | less movement |
| *piu mosso* | | more movement |

## Other musical terms

| | | |
|---|---|---|
| *staccato* | stacc. | detached, short (usually shown by a dot under or over the note) |
| *cantabile* | | in a singing style |
| *da capo* | D.C. | repeat from the beginning |
| *dal segno* | D.S. | repeat from the sign or repeat marks |
| *dolce* | | sweetly |
| *fine* | | the end or finish |
| *forte piano* | fp | loud, then soft |
| *sforzando* | sf | forcing, accented |
| *grazioso* | | gracefully |
| *leggiero* | | lightly |
| *tenuto* | ten. | held |

*8va* ————┐ (placed above the notes)   play an octave higher

*8va* ————┘ (placed under the notes)   play an octave lower

M.M. ♩ = 96                  96 crotchet beats in every minute

M.M. ♩ = 60                  60 minim beats in every minute
(M.M. means Maelzel's Metronome)

> placed under or over a note       accent that note

⌒ over a note, or ‿ under a note      pause

‖: and :‖               The music within these two signs is to be repeated. If the first sign is omitted, the music is repeated from the beginning.

♩ ⨍                 The note is to be given slight emphasis.

♩♩♩♩ ♩♩♩♩      Slurs over or under dots mean that the notes should be slightly detached, but not as much as with ordinary staccato dots.

♩ ♩    *staccatissimo*    The note is to be played as short as possible.

# Intervals

Frequent reference to the earlier picture of a keyboard will help throughout this section.

An interval is the distance between two notes, that is, the difference in pitch between them.

All intervals consists of two elements:
1 - How far away the notes are from each other, ie. the distance.
2 - The quality of the interval.

To find the **distance** is simple. Write down the names of both notes, fill in all the missing letters of the alphabet and then count the *total number of letters*. For example:

C      to      G

C    D E F    G

The total number of letters is five, therefore the interval is a *fifth*.

The **quality** of the interval needs equal precision in working out, but is also a simple process.

The quality of the interval is found by using the *major scale* of the *lower note* of the interval, regardless of the key of the music in which the interval occurs. The key signature of the music must be ignored and only that of the major scale of the lower note taken into consideration.

If the *upper* note is contained in the major scale of the lower note, the interval will be either **major** or **perfect**.
Perfect intervals are distances of 4ths, 5ths and octaves and sound complete and finished in themselves.

Major intervals are distances of 2nds, 3rds, 6ths and 7ths. The 3rds and 6ths are harmonically satisfying, but the 2nds and 7ths sound incomplete.

*Examples:*      A               B              C              D

Example A
As there are five letter-names involved (**C** to **G**), the interval is a 5th. To find the sort of interval, or its quality, the major scale of the lower note is used, that is the scale of C major. G *does* occur in that scale, so the interval is bound to be either major or perfect. Because it is a 5th, it is perfect; therefore the interval C to G is a perfect fifth.

Example B
By using the same process, it can be worked out that **C** to **A** is a major sixth.

Example C
Here the notes involved are **G** to **C**. Because the lower note is G, the major scale of G will be used for the calculation. The size of the interval is a 4th. To find the quality of the interval, the question must be asked whether C is contained in the major scale of G. As it is, the interval is bound to be either major or perfect. Because the distance is a 4th, the interval is a perfect fourth.

Example D
The notes are **G** to **F**, giving an interval of a 7th. However, the note F is *not* contained in the scale of G, as the 7th or leading note of the scale is F sharp. Therefore the interval cannot be a major seventh.

An interval that is a semitone *smaller* than major is **minor.**
An interval that is a semitone *smaller* than perfect is **diminished.**

By looking at the picture of the keyboard, it can be seen that G to F is a semitone *smaller* than G to F sharp. G to F sharp is a major seventh; as G to F is a semitone smaller it must be a *minor* seventh.

*Example E:*

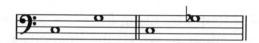

Both intervals are a fifth. As G appears in the major scale of C, the interval C to G is a perfect fifth. G flat does *not* appear in the major scale of C. By looking at the keyboard, it can be seen that the interval is a semitone smaller than that of C to G. An interval one semitone smaller than perfect is diminished, therefore **C** to **G flat** is a *diminished* fifth.

An interval that is a semitone *larger* than major or perfect is **augmented.**

*Examples:*    F                    G                    H                    J

Example F
**C to G sharp**  As stated in example E above, C to G is a perfect 5th. From the keyboard it can be seen that C to G sharp is a semitone larger, which will therefore make it an interval of an *augmented* fifth.

Example G
**F to B**  This is obviously a 4th. The major scale of F contains B flat. F to B is a semitone larger and is therefore an interval of an *augmented* fourth.

Examples H and J
By using the same process, it can be seen that example H is an augmented sixth and example J is an augmented third.

An interval which is a semitone *smaller* than minor or perfect is **diminished**.

*Example K:*

| | |
|---|---|
| C to E | is a major third because E is contained in the major scale of C. |
| C to E flat | is a minor third because it is a semitone smaller than a major third. |
| C to E double flat | is a diminished third because it is a semitone smaller than a minor third. |

*Example L:*

| | |
|---|---|
| C to G | is a perfect fifth. |
| C to G flat | is a diminished fifth. |
| F to B flat | is a perfect fourth. |
| F to B double flat | is a diminished fourth. |
| B to F sharp | is a perfect fifth. |
| B to F | is a diminished fifth. |

In all the minor, diminished and augmented intervals so far looked at, it is the top note which has been altered. If the top note is lowered, a major interval becomes minor and a minor or a perfect interval becomes diminished. If the top note is raised, a major or a perfect interval becomes augmented. However, an interval can be made smaller or larger by altering the lower note. If the lower note is raised, the interval becomes smaller; if it is lowered, the interval becomes larger.

*Example M:*

The interval **C sharp** to **F** is a fourth. The scale of C sharp major is used infrequently. Had the interval been C to F, the answer would have been easy, the interval being that of a perfect fourth. By raising the lower note from C to C sharp, the interval is a semitone smaller, therefore it is a diminished fourth.

*Example N:*

F flat to C  At first glance this appears immensely complicated. If the question is approached from the scale of F, the interval F to C is immediately apparent as being that of a perfect fifth. As the lower note has been flattened, making the interval a semitone larger, the interval F flat to C is an augmented fifth.


# Compound Intervals

Intervals are sometimes more than an octave apart and are known as **compound intervals**.

There are two ways to describe them and either is acceptable for examination purposes.
1 - By their true distance, that is the number of letter-names involved.
2 - By substituting the word *compound* for the first octave of the interval and then adding the correct interval that remains.

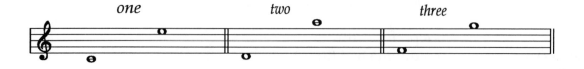

| | |
|---|---|
| *one* | a major 10<sup>th</sup>, or a compound major 3<sup>rd</sup> |
| *two* | a perfect 12<sup>th</sup>, or a compound perfect 5<sup>th</sup> |
| *three* | a major 9<sup>th</sup>, or a compound major 2<sup>nd</sup> |

Notice that intervals of 9<sup>ths</sup>, 10<sup>ths</sup>, 13<sup>ths</sup> and 14<sup>ths</sup> are major; 11<sup>ths</sup>, 12<sup>ths</sup> and 15<sup>ths</sup> are perfect.


# Inversion of Intervals

When the notes of *any* interval are turned upside-down, or inverted, the *size* will change. The *quality* of the interval will also change, except for perfect intervals. These remain perfect even when inverted.

A **major** interval when inverted will become a **minor** interval.
A **minor** interval when inverted will become a **major** interval.
A **diminished** interval when inverted will become an **augmented** interval.
An **augmented** interval when inverted will become a **diminished** interval.
A **perfect** interval when inverted will remain a **perfect** interval.

# Concords & discords

In everyday speech, concordant usually means *harmonious* or *agreeing with* and discordant usually means *quarrelsome* or *disagreeing with*. In music these words have equivalent, but precise, meanings.

**Concords** are of two sorts:

> **Perfect concords** are the *perfect* intervals of 4ths, 5ths and 8ths.
> **Imperfect concords** are the *major* and *minor* intervals of 3rds and 6ths.

Every other interval is a **discord**.
Discords are:

> major and minor 2nds and 7ths
> all augmented intervals
> all diminished intervals

The interval of an augmented 4th has an additional name of a **tritone**, because within this interval there are three tones.

Every major and harmonic minor scale has a tritone between the subdominant (4th) and leading note (7th).

# Further minor scales

Here are the remaining **harmonic** minor scales.

### C sharp harmonic minor

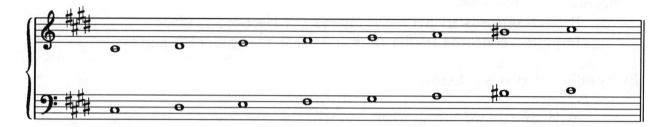

### G sharp harmonic minor

### D sharp harmonic minor

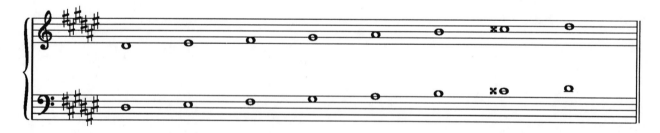

### A sharp harmonic minor

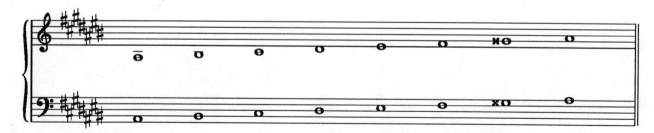

## F harmonic minor

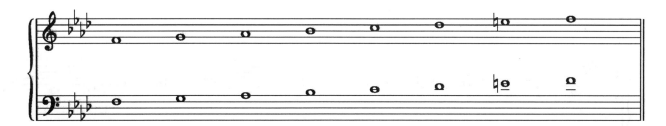

## B flat harmonic minor

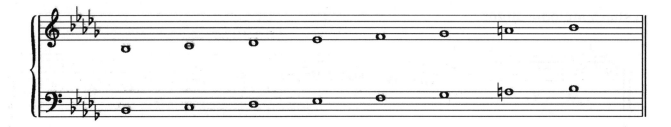

## E flat harmonic minor

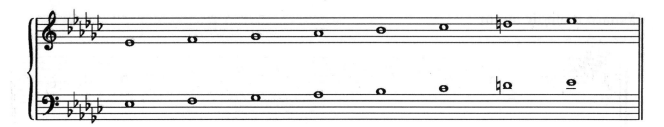

## A flat harmonic minor

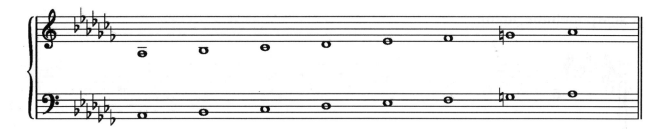

Here are the remaining **melodic** minor scales, both ascending and descending.

## C sharp melodic minor

## G sharp melodic minor

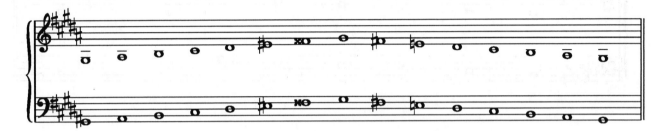

## D sharp melodic minor

## A sharp melodic minor

## F melodic minor

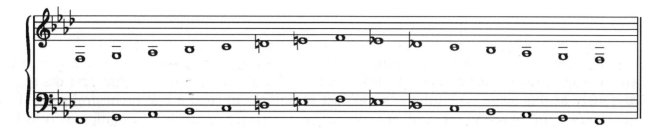

## B flat melodic minor

## E flat melodic minor

## A flat melodic minor

# Musical map reading

Learning the basic grammar and vocabulary of a language is only a beginning. In the same way that the words on a printed page convey the author's intentions, so the music on a printed page conveys the composer's intentions to anyone who is able to interpret the signs. Obviously at this stage no student can expect to be able to read a full orchestral score, but everyone should make an attempt, at every stage, to extract as much information as possible from whatever music they meet.

The questions below, after the musical examples, are intended as a guideline to the type of information a student should be looking for. This sort of analysis is often required in musical examinations.

**Example A**

| | |
|---|---|
| 1 | What does *Tempo di minuetto* mean? |
| 2 | What does the time signature mean? |
| 3 | Is this in simple or compound time? |
| 4 | Is the time duple, triple or quadruple? |
| 5 | The melody begins in D major. What key does it end in? |
| 6 | What does *p* under the first note mean? |
| 7 | What do the dots under notes in bar 6 mean? |
| 8 | What is the time name of the last note? |
| 9 | How many beats is the rest in the last bar worth? |

## Example B

1 What does *Vivace* mean?

2 Is the music in simple or compound time?

3 How many beats are in a bar?

4 State whether the music is in duple, triple or quadruple time.

5 What is the ornament in the second bar? (*Refer to page 64.*)

6 What is the accidental in bar 5?

7 Give the name of the fourth note in bar 11.

8 Choose one word from the following to describe the mood of this music: *dolente, mesto, tranquillo, spiritoso*

## Answers

*Example A*    1 - In the time of a minuet 2 - three crotchet beats in a bar 3 - simple
         4 - triple 5 - A major 6 - quietly 7 - short, detached 8 - minim 9 - one

*Example B*    1 - lively 2 - compound 3 - two 4 - duple 5 - acciaccatura 6 - natural
         7 - B natural 8 - spiritoso

# The Chromatic Scale

Every note in a chromatic scale is just a semitone away from its neighbour, therefore every octave contains twelve semitones. To produce the chromatic scale on a keyboard, all the black notes as well as all the white notes in the octave are used. The scale can be formed on any note.

Chromatic means *colourful*. Certainly when notes are introduced which are not contained in the key of the music the sound becomes more colourful, or *coloured*. The resulting sound is more interesting.

There are two ways of writing this scale.

**Melodic Notation**
Here the notes are sharpened when ascending and flattened when descending in order to form the series of semitones. This notation is simple to understand and economical in its use of accidentals.

**The Harmonic Chromatic Scale**
In this version the notation is approached harmonically, that is, bearing in mind the way in which every note relates to the tonic. The process for constructing this scale is as follows:

Taking **C** as the starting-point, the scale of C major is written:

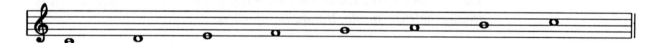

The notes which are different in the C minor scale are added.

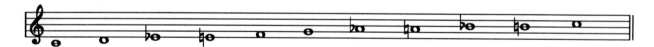

Notice that the 3rd, 6th and 7th notes now need accidentals because of the addition of the notes of the minor scale.

Only two semitones are missing: namely that between **C** and **D** and that between **F** and **G**. Between **C** and **D**, **D flat** is used; between **F** and **G**, **F sharp** is used, because these two notes are contained in the formation of some of the more *colourful* chords in this key. The same notes are used both ascending and descending and great care must be taken in the descending version to ensure that the correct accidentals are used.

The complete harmonic chromatic scale looks like this:

There is an easy way to build the harmonic chromatic scale. By looking carefully at the above example, it can be seen that every note is used twice except for the tonic and the dominant, the two most important notes in any scale.

**Step 1**   Write the tonic, the dominant and the higher tonic. If the scale is descending as well as ascending, the dominant and the lower tonic need to be added:

**Step 2**   Write every other note in twice:

**Step 3**   Add any accidentals needed to make this into a chromatic scale, that is, a scale in which every note is a semitone away from its neighbour:

These steps apply regardless of the starting note.

In the example above, the notes marked * are already sharpened by the accidentals used when ascending. These accidentals do not need to be repeated, provided that no bar line has been inserted.

When beginning on a flattened note, extra attention must be given to the accidentals. The above three steps must still be strictly observed. This gives rise to the necessity for using double flats and, as the next note will have only one flat, the correct means of cancellation has to be maintained. (Refer to page 19.) The following example illustrates this point.

# Alto and Tenor Clefs
## (The C clef)

In addition to the bass and treble clefs, the **C clef** is also used.

Unlike the 𝄞 (**G**) and 𝄢 (**F**) clefs, which are fixed, the 𝄡 (**C**) clef is movable.

Whichever line goes through the middle of the sign is middle C. When middle C is on the third line, this is called the **alto clef** and when it is on the fourth line it is called the **tenor clef**.

The reason for these clefs is to avoid writing an excessive number of ledger lines. In early music the alto clef was used for the alto line and the tenor clef for the tenor line in choral works although this practice has now been discontinued. It has become customary to use the alto clef for the viola and the tenor clef for the higher notes of the cello, bassoon and tenor trombone.

In exactly the same way as the lines and spaces of the bass and treble clefs have to be learnt, so the same method of memorization will be necessary. The reward will be the ability to read the music of any instrument in an orchestral score. Again, the writing of words in these two clefs will help, as was shown on page 4.

The lines of the alto clef are       F  A   C   E   G
The spaces of the alto clef are      G   B   D   F

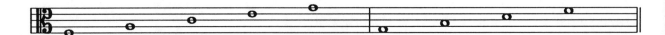

The lines of the tenor clef are      D   F   A   C   E
The spaces of the tenor clef are     E   G   B   D

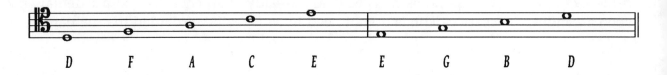

D      F      A      C      E      E      G      B      D

# How to write a rhythm to words

Writing a rhythm to words is the very first step in composing a song.

As discussed on page 5, all music has a pulse or beat, giving life and form to it, rather like the bones in a body. Living things without bones, such as jelly-fish, have no definite shape; animals, including humans, have a skeleton of bones which give a very definite shape. The pulse throbs through music and it is this factor which gives it its energy and quality of being alive. Some pulses are stronger than others, for example, on the first beat of the bar.

Words, too, have a rhythm. Some syllables are strong, others weaker, and some are very faint indeed. When writing a rhythm to words, one thing has to take precedence over everything else: **The strong accents of the music and the strong accents of the words should be in the same place.** If this is achieved, the result will be like a shoe or a glove which fits perfectly. If the *strong* accent of the music is placed with the *weak* accent of the words, or vice versa, it feels like a glove worn on the wrong hand, or a shoe on the wrong foot.

Occasionally - once in a song, or perhaps not at all - a word needs special treatment. That *may* be an occasion for separating the strong accents, but it is rather like using herbs in cooking: a little may improve, but a lot can ruin! In every *good* song, most of the strong accents of both the words and the music co-incide, whether the tempo is slow, moderate or fast, ensuring that it has shape and that it feels right. Consideration of the separation of the accents is not within the scope of this book. It is first necessary to get the basics right.

The process for achieving success, as with most of the processes connected with music, is straightforward providing the basic rules are adhered to. There are only problems when an alternative method or a short cut is attempted.

For example, to write a rhythm to the following words:

> *I wandered lonely as a cloud*
> *That floats on high o'er vale and hill.*

## Step 1
Write out the words, dividing them into separate syllables, spacing them out in order to give room to work. Do not try to circumvent this step or you are likely to end up with syllables without notes.

> *I    wan  -  dered    lone  -  ly    as    a    cloud*
> *That    floats    on    high    o'er    vale    and    hill.*

Remember that in writing a *rhythm*, every syllable will need one note; when composing a *tune*, some syllables might have more than one note, perhaps several.

**Step 2**

Re-write the individual syllables, this time allowing at least a gap of one line in which to write the notes between the two lines of poetry:

*I wan - dered lone - ly as a cloud*

*That floats on high o'er vale and hill.*

(In practice, these two steps are usually combined.)

**Step 3**

The words initially need to be spoken aloud in order to find their strong accents. It is worth remembering that the way in which words are pronounced is generally fixed. If the accents of the words and the music are to be brought together, the *word* accents must first be located. Once the first line is said aloud, the stressed syllables are easily found. In this particular case, the emphasis is on *wan, lone, as* and *cloud*.

**Step 4**

Mark these stressed syllables as follows:

*I wan - dered lone - ly as a cloud*

**Step 5**

Because the first beat is the strongest beat of the bar, the strong accents in music come immediately *after* the bar-line. Therefore put a bar-line *before* every stressed syllable.

*I |wan - dered | lone - ly | as a | cloud*

This gives a clear idea of the shape of the bar.

**Step 6**

The next stage is to select a time-signature. There is never just one time-signature to any given rhythm. Once the accents are sorted satisfactorily two, three or four beats in a bar can usually be selected and there is often a choice between simple or compound time. The time-signature is really governed by the composer's preference, together with the rhythm and mood of the words. To illustrate this point, look at the following three examples:

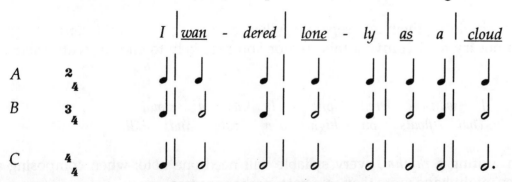

All three fit, because the accents of the words and music come in the same place in all three examples.

## Step 7 - Imagination

The previous examples were correct, but predictable and possibly boring. The rhythm needs to be made more varied and interesting. This can be done by varying the lengths of notes according to the importance of the words and the way in which they are pronounced, whilst still maintaining the **correct accents**.

When saying the word *lonely*, it is natural to linger on *lone*, giving less to *-ly*. Only in example B was that done with the note-values, but it can be done equally easily in example A:

*lone - ly*

and example C:

Every bar needs to be considered in the same way, always remembering that music *must* have variety.

Consider the following versions:

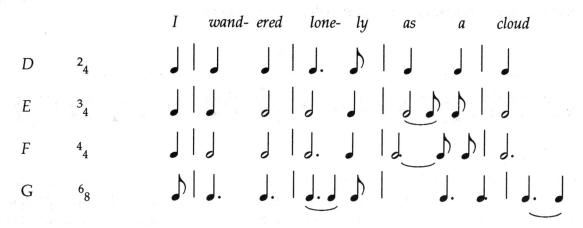

They have variety and interest, but in every example the accents of the words and music are in the same place.

# Writing a musical reply to a given phrase

Some examination boards simply call this "adding an answering phrase". A very loose definition of 'phrase' is 'an incomplete sentence'. So this section could be called *Completing a Musical Sentence* or *Adding an Answer to a Question*. It is a fascinating exercise and another step on the road to composing a melody.

In speech, words can be grouped together to make a phrase or a sentence. In the same way, music divides not only into bars, but into larger groups of several bars, in order to make a musical **phrase**. Usually, two bars or a multiple of two will make up a phrase, although in practice four is the most widely-used number of bars.

A complete sentence consists of more than one phrase, thereby achieving a feeling of balance. For example, "Today is a lovely day," is a complete statement, but in some instances would only be half of a sentence, as in, "Today is a lovely day, so we will go for a picnic." This provides an **answering** phrase to the first part of the sentence.

Similarly, some musical phrases need to be answered. This well-known tune contains three separate phrases, which together make a complete musical sentence:

This illustrates how phrases build into a musical sentence. The rest of this section deals with adding only *one* answering phrase, so the musical sentences will all consist of two phrases. Musical sentences, as shown above, may contain more than two phrases; that can be dealt with at leisure when the skill of adding a single answering phrase has been acquired.

Exactly as in speech, a musical sentence needs to feel *balanced*. This can easily be achieved when talking by altering the speed with which the words are said. When speaking, pace is left to the speaker. Some people speak very quickly, others very slowly; most people speak at a moderate pace. In music, there is not the same freedom. The composer indicates the tempo and the number of beats in a bar; those factors are not negotiable. Therefore the way to achieve balance in a musical sentence is to make the reply the same number of bars as the opening statement. At this stage, the opening statement is usually four bars, so the reply should also be four bars.

Start by looking carefully at the opening statement and at the way in which it is constructed. It may be possible to use a particular rhythm or group of notes from it. Alternatively, it may be decided to use something completely different: instead of the notes falling or rising, as in the opening phrase, they might go in the opposite direction. The possibilities are endless.

There are certain characteristics which will always apply:

1.      The sense of *balance* is of paramount importance, therefore the reply should be the same length as the opening.
2.      The musical sentence must be *complete* in itself in order to feel satisfactory. Regardless of where the opening statement led, the reply should be brought back to the tonic, or to a note of the tonic chord.
3.      Material from the opening may be used if it lends itself to this.

Many students have been known to simply repeat the opening phrase except for the last note, which they change into the tonic. This does nothing to improve the musical skills of the student and becomes a useless exercise.

Someone is sure to quote famous composers whose answering phrase consisted of the first statement with an altered last note. Beethoven did it in the last movement of his Ninth Symphony:

Admittedly it gives a perfectly balanced answering phrase, but Beethoven could have written thousands of answering phrases. Surely at this point the student's task is to learn how to write with variety.

In the following answering phrases, different ways of illustrating the above rules are shown.

### 1 - Balance
In example A the answering phrase is shorter than the beginning. It simply does not *feel* like a correct reply. In example B the phrases are of equal length.

*Example A*

*Example B*

## 2 - Making the sentence complete

Example C finishes on a note not in the scale. Example D finishes on the tonic as suggested.

*Example C*

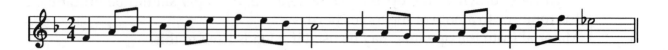

*Example D*

## 3 - Using material from the given statement

The overall pattern of the **rhythm** is ♩ ♪♪ which could be continued by using the same rhythm. Alternatively it could be reversed to become ♪♪ ♩ as in the following example.

*Example E*

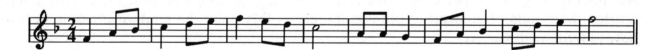

The **pitch** pattern uses adjacent, or next-door notes, except between the first two notes, **F** and **A**, where there is a jump of a third. The pitch rises at the beginning and falls at the end.

In the first example the answering phrase follows that pattern, but begins one tone higher, on **G** instead of **F**.

*Example F*

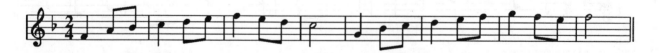

This is acceptable because it is melodic. Many composers have written in a similar way; but it is not an exercise to tax anyone's musicianship. It could just as easily have been written by an unmusical person.

The most obvious alteration is to use the notes from example F, but with the rhythm of example E.

*Example G*

A further variation might be made by introducing contrary motion - when the first phrase goes up in pitch the answer can go down, and vice versa.

*Example H*

At this point, decisions have to be made as to how to finish. If the contrary motion idea is retained, the last two bars could look like this:

*Example H(a)*        *Example H(b)*

Example H(a) ends on the dominant and is acceptable because that note is also found in the tonic chord. Generally, though, the ending is stronger if it finishes on the tonic, as in example H(b).

In example H(b), although the intervals and distances between the notes are altered, the contrary motion is still maintained.

In example H(c) the contrary motion idea is abandoned at the end of bar 6 and the tune is completed with the lower tonic. The following are some possible ideas, but others could be perfectly acceptable. In this sort of work there is never just *one* correct idea; provided the rules are observed there could be many satisfactory answers.

*Example H(c)*

More endings could be devised, but these examples should illustrate the numerous and varied ways in which material can be used.

# Transposition

To transpose a piece of music means to change the pitch at which it is written, either by making it higher or lower. In most cases, this will result in a change of key. To be able to transpose is a useful skill, especially for singers, who so often hear a song which they would like to sing, but find that it is in the wrong key for their particular voice. Transposition is well within the reach of anyone who has a secure knowledge of intervals, as will be shown in the rest of this section.

*Example A*

*Example B*

*Example C*

In *example A*, the first four bars of "Twinkle Twinkle Little Star" are in the key of F. In *example B* the same music is written one tone higher and in *example C* one tone lower. Although the tune was played in a higher key in *example B* and a lower one in *example C*, the tune did not change. This was because the intervals between the notes remained the same throughout the three examples. It is only the *pitch* that has altered, *not the tune*. This is probably the most important fact to remember when transposing: **the tune remains the same**.

The simplest sort of transposition is to make the pitch of the music an octave higher or lower.

*Example D*

This example is in the key of **C**; however many octaves up or down it is transposed, the key will still be **C**, so there is no need to discover the new key signature. In order to transpose this example *up* an octave, the process is as follows:

Write the clef and the time signature. Find the new starting note, ie. the note that is an octave *above* middle C, the original starting note. This is the beginning of the transposition.

Just as the first note was transposed an octave higher, so all the succeeding notes need to be transposed an octave higher. It is easier at this stage to number the notes.

1   2   3   4   5   6   7   8   9   10   11   12   13   14

The *second* note in the transposition needs to be an octave higher than the second note in the original; the *third* note an octave higher than the third note in the original; and so on through the fourteen notes. By keeping the intervals the same, the same tune will be written at a higher pitch. The transposed version will look like this:

*Example E*

*Example E* shows the same tune, this time written in the bass clef. To transpose it an octave lower, the process is the same. Because the interval of transposition is an octave, the key will still be C. Put the clef, time signature and the first note on the stave. By keeping all the intervals the same distance from each other, the finished transposition will look like this:

Here is *example D* again. The next step is to transpose it an octave lower using a *different* clef.

As before, put the correct clef and time signature in. Because the interval of transposition is an octave, there will be no change of key signature.

Find the starting note. One octave below middle C using the bass clef will be C on the second space. The process now is to keep the *same* interval between each pair of notes. The finished transposition will look like this:

**Page 57**

To transpose a melody written in the bass clef an octave higher using the treble clef the process is exactly the same. *Example F* shows the same four bars of music, but in the key of **G**.

*Example F*

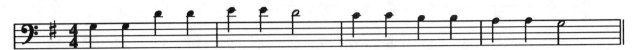

Put in the clef, the key-signature and the time-signature. The key-signature and time-signature will be the same, but the clef will change from the bass to the treble.

Place the starting note one octave above where it is written in the bass clef. This will be on the second line of the treble clef. Complete the transposition by keeping the interval between each pair of notes the same. The completed transposition will look like this:

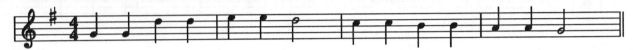

To transpose a melody an interval other than an octave, the process is the same, but greater checking is needed. To transpose *example D* a tone higher - that is, an interval of a **major second** - steps one to seven need to be completed.

**Step 1**   First establish the key in which the original is written, otherwise it will be impossible to find the key of the transposed version. Here the original is in C Major.

**Step 2**   A major second higher than C is D, so it needs to be transposed into the key of **D Major**.

**Step 3**   Write in the clef, then the key-signature of D Major, which has **F** and **C** sharps.

**Step 4**   Add the time-signature.

**Step 5**   Find the first note. It must be a **major second** higher than middle C, which is **D**.

**Step 6**   Complete the exercise by adding the other notes, keeping each note a major second higher than the corresponding note in the original. (For convenience the notes are numbered.)

The 1<sup>st</sup> note is D. The 2<sup>nd</sup> note is the same. The 3<sup>rd</sup> note of the original is G; a major second higher than G is A, so the 3<sup>rd</sup> note in the transposed version will go in the second space. The 4<sup>th</sup> note is the same as the 3<sup>rd</sup>.

The 5<sup>th</sup> and 6<sup>th</sup> notes are both A in the original. A major second higher will be B. The 7<sup>th</sup> note of the original is G. A major second higher will be A.

The 8<sup>th</sup> & 9<sup>th</sup> notes are originally both F. A major second higher will be G. The 10<sup>th</sup> & 11<sup>th</sup> notes are on E. A major second higher will give F sharp. Originally, the 12<sup>th</sup> & 13<sup>th</sup> notes were on D; a major second higher will be E. The 14<sup>th</sup> note was on C; a major second higher will be D. The completed transposition will look like this:

**Step 7**   This transposition was worked out by transposing every note a major second higher, that is vertically. The transposition can also be worked out horizontally, that is by checking the intervals between each pair of notes and making sure that the same interval is retained in the transposed version. In the early stages, it is sensible to use *both* methods.

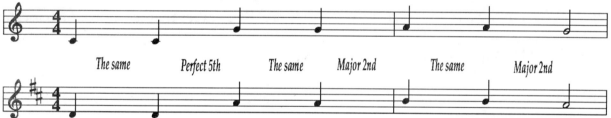

Any interval of transposition, either higher or lower, can be worked out provided these steps are adhered to. Do not omit any step - accuracy in transposition depends on precision in completing the seven steps which are set out below.

**Step 1**   Establish the key of the original.

**Step 2**   Establish the new key.

**Step 3**   Write in the clef and the new key-signature.

**Step 4**   Add the time-signature.

**Step 5**   Find and add the first note.

**Step 6**   Add all the other notes, maintaining the correct interval from the corresponding note in the original.

**Step 7**   Check horizontally the intervals between each pair of notes.

Here is *example D*.

To transpose this down a **major third** follow *exactly* the seven steps involved. This should result in:

So far only the same clef has been used. To transpose to a different clef presents no additional difficulties, but it should be ensured that the first note is in the correct place in the new clef. To transpose the example just completed down a **minor third** into the bass clef, proceed as follows:

**Step 1**   Establish the key of the original - A♭ major.

**Step 2**   Establish the new key. A minor third lower than A♭ is **F**, so the new key will be **F major**.

**Step 3**   Write in the clef and the new key-signature. Remember that it will be the bass clef.

**Step 4**   Add the time-signature.

**Step 5**   Find out and add the first note. A minor third below A♭ is **F**, and this will be placed on the fourth line of the stave.

**Steps 6 and 7**   These are the same as before, always remembering that the bass clef is being used.

The completed transposition should look like this.

The examples so far have only contained notes which were in the original scale; in other words there were no accidentals. When accidentals *are* present they do not present a problem provided a knowledge of intervals is applied. Here is *example D* with three notes altered by accidentals.

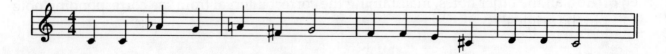

To transpose this a minor third higher, first complete steps 1 to 5 which remain unchanged. Complete step 6 as if there were no accidentals.

The original has accidentals before the 3rd, 5th, 6th and 11th notes. The transposed version will therefore require accidentals before these same notes. **If there is an accidental in the original, there MUST be an accidental in the same place in the transposed version; otherwise the tune will be wrong.** It will not necessarily be the same accidental as in the original, so the right accidental must be ascertained.

The 3rd note in the original was A flat; when transposed an accidental is needed to lower the C natural to C flat .
The 5th note was originally A natural and so in the transposed version C natural will be required, to make it a minor third higher.

Some people would argue that the accidental before this 5th note is superfluous because accidentals last only for the duration of the bar. However, composers like to make their intentions clear and unambiguous. Especially in compositions involving several lines of music such use of the accidental avoids confusion. In transposition, stick to the rule: **if an accidental appears in the original, there must be a corresponding accidental in the transposed version.**

In the original version, the 6th note is an F sharp but in the transposed version there is an A flat which is an interval of a *diminished* third. As the music is being transposed a minor third higher an accidental is needed to raise it by a semitone. This illustrates how different accidentals are needed in order to produce the same effect.

The completed transposition, with the remaining notes worked out by the same process, looks like this:

In a correct transposition the *tune* will always sound the same. It is only the *pitch* which has changed. If the original tune is in a major key, any transposed version will also be in a major key, otherwise it will sound wrong. Conversely, if the original tune is in a minor key, any transposed version will also be in a minor key.

# Syncopation

Barlines divide up the notes into bars. Music normally falls into two or three beats in a bar, or multiples of those numbers.

The pulse or beat gives a stress - the quality that makes you want to tap your foot or clap your hands. The beat with the strongest stress comes immediately after the barline, no matter what the time signature is. With four beats in a bar there will be a secondary stress on the third beat, not as heavy as on the first beat, but more than on the second or fourth beats. This gives the *feel* to the bar. These stresses or accents are all normal and in the right place.

When music is syncopated, the accents have been transferred to a different part of the bar, or even to a different part of the beat. The word **syncopation** could be defined as being when any irregularity of accent or stress has the effect of contradicting the normal rhythm. This effect is not always obvious from looking at a piece of music; the effect needs to be heard and felt, as well as seen.

There are various ways of producing syncopation and transmitting that exact effect into the written note.

**Example 1**
The accents on the weak part of the beat produce syncopation because in normal musical experience the strong accent is on the *first* of any group of notes.

**Example 2**
A rest never has an accent; it cannot because it is a silence. In this example, rests are on the strong, beginning part of the beat and the notes come on the normally weak part.

**Example 3**
The strongest beat of the bar, as already said, is on the first beat. Here, a weak beat at the end of the bar is tied over the bar-line, thereby moving that strong accent which normally occurs there to a weaker part of the bar.

**Example 4**
In this example, notes are put in between beats.

Syncopation can be found in Western Music of all musical periods from the 13th Century onwards. It is particularly prominent in African and Black American music, and was hugely important in the development of Ragtime and Jazz.

# Ornaments

The whole question of ornaments appears to be one of 'insurmountable difficulty'. There are many reasons for this. Everyone seems either to 'work out' their ornaments differently, or not to be able to work them out at all. The same ornament is different in different periods of music. Just remembering them can make it seem as though you need a degree in mathematics. This is a sad and very unnecessary state of affairs. By remembering a few basic rules, ornaments can be dealt with in a very straightforward way.

First: what is an ornament? It is something which embellishes, beautifies or adorns. So - far from frightening the living daylights out of a musician - it is there to add decoration and enhancement to what is already on the page of music.

In earlier times there was a practical use for ornaments in keyboard music, because the keyboard instruments had so little sustaining power. To decorate a note (ie. to add an ornament to it) reminded our ears of what the note was, a useful alternative to the sustaining pedal of the modern piano. But the music for other instruments and for singing also contained a great deal of ornamentation, so we must deduce that the function was primarily to make the playing or singing more expressive.

Many people have written about ornaments and many editions of music suggest slightly different versions. What is the *correct* way? This is almost impossible to answer because so many different factors affect ornaments. The date and country of origin of the music, and the speed at which the composer indicated that it should be performed are just three influences. However, there are some general rules to apply, and these are given as appropriate to each of the five main ornaments.

## The Appoggiatura

The word comes from the Italian *appogiare* - to lean, to prop or support. It is written as a small note slurred to a full-sized note:

As far as the melody is concerned, the appoggiatura is as important as the main note, and it is given *half* the value of the main note. The example above would be written out in full as:

When it is written before a dotted note and joined to it, it is given two-thirds of the value of the note:

Sometimes an appoggiatura is placed before a chord. Then it takes its value from the *upper* note of the chord.

## The Acciaccatura

Also called a 'crushed' note. This is a terrible word to spell: remember it contains four Cs. It comes from the Italian word *acciaccare* - to crush, bruise or pound. The last meaning is unfortunate, especially when applied to pianists. The common interpretation is 'to crush'.

Some authorities suggest that this is really a short appoggiatura, and that in earlier music - eg. of the Baroque period - it formed a dissonance in the chord.

The accepted principle of the acciaccatura - in keeping its character of a *crushed* note - is that it should be played as quickly as possible before the note to which it is attached. If requested to write it out, it is sensible to make it a demisemiquaver:

Note two things:

    The acciaccatura is written with the tail pointing upwards.

    The difference between the appoggiatura ♪ and the acciaccatura ♪ . Check for the small line across the tail to make sure that it is an acciaccatura.

## Mordent

This ornament can cause confusion, because at different times in musical history it appeared to mean different things. The name is derived from the Italian *mordente*, meaning 'to bite' - a very apt description.

On earlier keyboard instruments it was not possible to vary the volume in the way pianists can on a modern piano. A note could not be accented. Therefore, if a composer wanted to draw attention to a note, a mordent would frequently be placed over it, thereby commanding the listener's attention. This practice was common until the Baroque period, but a mordent at that time was interpreted differently from the way in which it would be in today.

What appears to have been the original mordent is now known as an *inverted, or lower mordent*. What is commonly called a mordent today would more precisely be called an *upper mordent*.

An upper mordent is shown as: ∿    An inverted, or lower mordent is shown as: ∿

Both mordents consist of three notes. In the upper mordent the main note, the note *above* it and the main note again are played rhythmically, the first two notes usually being played as demisemiquavers, the third note taking the rest of the value of the original note.

So if a mordent is placed over a crochet the first two notes will each be a demisemiquaver, which will leave a dotted quaver for the third note:

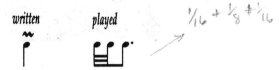

Similarly, if a mordent is placed over a dotted crotchet, it will sound:

If placed over a minim, it will sound:

An inverted, or lower, mordent consists of the main note, the note *below* it and the main note. The rhythm is exactly the same for both upper and lower mordents.

If an accidental is placed above an upper mordent, this requires the upper note to be altered as directed.

If an accidental is placed *below* an inverted or lower mordent, the middle note is altered in the same way.

In neither case is the rhythmic shape altered.

In the Baroque period an extended, or 'Double' mordent was used. It was indicated by lengthening the sign and it was played as follows:

## The Turn

The sign for a turn is :  ∾

This is a four-note ornament which consists of the note above the main note, the main note, the note below the main note, and then the main note again. If a turn is placed above **C**, the notes played would be **D C B C**.

The way in which the lengths of the notes are decided depend on a number of factors, but there are a few general rules to follow.

When a turn is placed over a crotchet, or a note of shorter value, in music with a moderate to fast tempo, it can be divided into four equal notes. When it is placed over a minim, the turn is played as shown below.

However, if the tempo is slow to moderate, it is perfectly correct for the turn to take up *half* of the value of the crotchet; the last note of the turn will be given the remainder of the time-value of the original note. When the turn is placed over a minim at this tempo, it is played as shown below.

Compare this with the illustration above. Only the tempo has changed, but the sound is very different.

# The inverted turn can be written in two ways:

It is really an *up-side-down* turn, ie. the note below the main note, the main note, the note above, and then the main note again. An inverted turn on the note **C** consists of **B C D C**. Compare this with the first sentence of this section. The rules for the lengths of notes *in every instance* are the same for inverted turns as for turns.

## Turns placed after a note

When a turn is *over* a note, only four notes are involved, but when a turn comes *after* a note, five notes are involved because the main note is played *as well as* the four notes of the turn.

Turns placed after an ordinary note - crotchet, quaver, etc - *usually* follow quite a simple rule. In moderately to fast-paced music, divide the note into two. The first half is given to the note *before* the turn; the second half is divided into four, and this accommodates the four notes of the turn. These four notes will be the four *around* the principal note. Now this sounds much more complicated than it actually is, until broken down into simple steps:

1   Divide the crochet **G** into two. That gives ♪♪
    Give the first quaver to the main note, **G**.

2   Divide the second quaver into four, ie. 4 demisemiquavers.

3   Give one of these demisemiquavers to each note of the turn. The turn around **G** will be **A G F G**.

4   Put the two together and then play on.

If these steps are adhered to, the turns will sound accurate and neat. Here are a few examples:

In slow to moderately-paced music, it may sound more musical to give longer to the first note so that the turn sounds graceful within that slow tempo, eg:

In this example the first, principal note was given three-quarters of its value, the turn being played in one-quarter of the time.

In music of earlier periods it was automatically assumed that the notes of the scale of the piece of music would be used for the turn. More recently, the composer sometimes indicates otherwise.

If an accidental is placed *above* a turn, you give that accidental to the upper note, ie. the note *above* the main note. Similarly, if an accidental is placed *below* the turn, you give that accidental to the note *below* the main note. This rule applies to inverted turns in exactly the same way.

## The turn after a dotted note

Where a turn is placed after a *dotted* note, the process is as follows:

1    Divide the note into three: ♪ ♪ ♪
                                 x   y   z

2    Give the first quaver (**x**) to the principal note:

3    The first three notes of the turn must fit equally into the second quaver (**y**), ie. they will be **triplet** semiquavers. The first 3 notes of the turn are: the note above, the main note & the note below.

4    The last quaver (**z**) will be given to the final note of the turn:

5    Group the notes correctly. The beat is a crochet. There are three beats in a bar.

This shows the correct grouping.

The rules apply to all lengths of dotted notes. Inverted turns are treated in exactly the same way. Accidentals are incorporated as previously shown.

# The Trill or Shake

Of all ornaments, this probably has the greatest number of variations and possible interpretations. At its simplest, it is an instruction to play rapidly the note beneath the trill sign and the note above alternately for the length of the given note. If a trill sign is put above C, which is a crochet, you would play **C D C D C D** etc for the duration of that crochet, *ending on* C, that being the main note.

Through the centuries, three signs have been used to indicate a trill: *tr* or + or ∿ (the latter being the sign of the extended mordent discussed earlier.) The first sign has been in general use since the late eighteenth century. Sometimes it is followed by a wavy line after the sign which may mark the length of the trill, eg.

The way in which trills are performed varies in several ways, and both instrumentalists and singers need to be able to execute them. If asked to write a trill as it would be played, it is normally written out with more or less equal notes. When performing, artists sometimes vary this, perhaps by beginning slowly and gradually getting faster.

However, the main differences occur at the start and the finish of the trill. The tempo of the music governs the number of notes which can be played. In music up to and including Haydn and Mozart, the trill begins on the upper note. In later music, the trill begins on the main note. Whether the trill starts on the written note or the upper note, whether the pace is fast or slow, the trill will *always* end on the written note.

In music where the pace is slow to moderate, the notes of the trill are likely to be demisemiquavers. In fast music the notes would more likely be semiquavers. A modern trill will start and finish on the written note, but this gives an odd number of notes. Therefore a triplet sign is placed over three of the notes, indicating that they should be played in the time of two, as in the following example:

Many performers find it more musical to make the ending of a trill into a turn. The last four notes would then be **E D C D** and it would be written out as follows:

If the tempo were fast, it might be possible only to play semiquavers, eg:

As stated earlier, in music up to and including Haydn and Mozart the trill begins on the upper note, with one exception, giving an even number of notes and doing away with the need for a triplet. The exception occurs where the *upper* note of the trill is the same as the previous note. In this case, the trill begins on the main note. A turn, as explained above, is usual on the last four notes and it could be indicated in several ways. It might be written in full-sized notes, or it might be written as **grace notes**. (These are ornamental notes shown in small type which are additional to the total value of notes in the bar. Appoggiaturas and acciaccaturas are examples. Composers such as as Chopin sometimes used groups of two or more grace notes.) However, it is usual to complete the trill with a turn even when *not* indicated. The note values of the turn are the same as those of the trill.

In music from Beethoven to today, if a composer wants the trill to begin on the upper note he will put an acciaccatura on that upper note before the main note, eg:

When the note with the trill is the same as the previous note, the trill invariably begins on the upper note, eg:

# Chords

The Oxford Dictionary defines a chord as a group of notes sounded together. Perhaps the statement *three or more notes sounded together* might be clearer. In Western music **melody** - the tune - is associated with the underlying **harmony** - the chords to which the notes of melody belong - without even thinking about it, because in this type of music these two elements are virtually inseparable.

The triad is the basis of all chord formation. It can be formed on every note of the scale and the individual triads are referred to by the degree of the scale on which each is built.

For example, in the scale of C major:

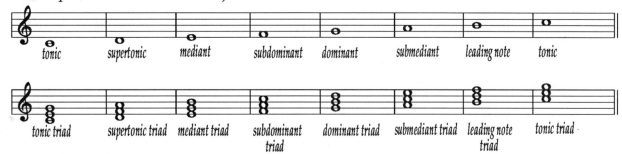

A quick and universally understood way of indicating a chord is to use Roman numerals:

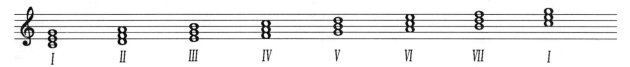

The different positions of the triad can be shown by using a small letter at the side of the Roman numeral:

eg.    Chord I        in Root position         is shown by  **Ia**
       Chord I        in 1st inversion         is shown by  **Ib**
       Chord I        in 2nd inversion         is shown by  **Ic**

and    Chord IV       in Root position         is shown by  **IVa**
       Chord V        in 1st inversion         is shown by  **Vb**
       Chord VI       in 2nd inversion         is shown by  **VIc**

and so on.

One point can be somewhat confusing. The notes described as the root, 3rd & 5th of the chord are maintained regardless of the position of the chord, eg.

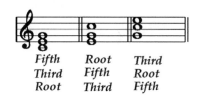

Fifth    Root     Third
Third    Fifth    Root
Root     Third    Fifth

In the C major triad, **C** is the root, **E** is the 3<sup>rd</sup> and **G** is the 5<sup>th</sup>, whether in root position, 1<sup>st</sup> or 2<sup>nd</sup> inversion.

It can also be seen from this how the shape of the chord alters. The triad in root position consists of two intervals, each of a 3<sup>rd</sup>, **C to E** and **E to G**.
In the inversions there is an interval of a 3<sup>rd</sup>, **E to G** and an interval of a 4<sup>th</sup>, **G to C**.

Often in examinations - even in very low grades - students are asked to write the **TONIC TRIAD** of a given key, sometimes with key signature, sometimes without. This is simply the TRIAD formed on the TONIC of the requested scale, ie. the root, with the 3<sup>rd</sup> and 5<sup>th</sup> above. When writing a triad without the key signature, it is crucial to add any necessary accidentals, eg. G major does not need any accidentals; D major certainly does, or the tonic triad of D minor is produced.

Refer to page 21 and Appendix 1 for the tonic triads in all major and minor keys.

It is a very simple matter to find the first & second inversions of any of these major or minor tonic triads. A few examples will demonstrate:

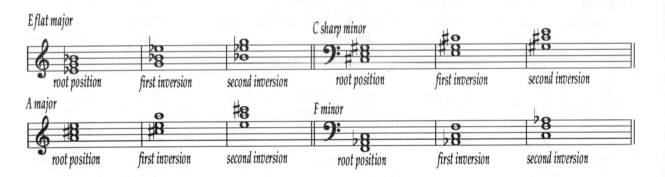

Only tonic triads have been looked at in detail so far, but a triad can be formed on any and every note of the scale.

The astonishing and yet simple fact of chords, all of which begin life as some form of a triad, is that from a musical point of view they do not function in isolation, but relate to each other. As in a family, some members have a greater rapport between them than others, although all are related; so in music, some chords will follow each other perfectly, while others sound a little uneasy.

Obviously, the most important chord, or triad, in any key is the tonic, which forms the home base. Next in importance will be the triad on the dominant; then the triad on the sub-dominant. These three chords - in any key - form the basis for much of the harmony in many tunes. The chords on the supertonic and the sub-mediant are used to give variety and interest.

In the early stages of chordal work, or **harmony** to use its musical name, the chords on the mediant and leading note are to be avoided. Extra rules apply to them and therefore they present extra difficulties.

There are **four** different types of triads: **major, minor, augmented** and **diminished**

A **major** triad is one which contains a **major 3rd** and a **perfect 5th**
A **minor** triad is one which contains a **minor 3rd** and a **perfect 5th**
An **augmented** triad is one which contains a **major 3rd** and an **augmented 5th**
A **diminished** triad is one which contains a **minor 3rd** and a **diminished 5th**

Both intervals in each triad are calculated from the root: the root to the 3rd and the root to the 5th. As the following examples will show, this is not nearly as complicated as it sounds. All these triads are built on middle C:

| | | | |
|---|---|---|---|
| *Example A* | a **major** triad | C to E (major 3rd) | C to G (perfect 5th) |
| *Example B* | a **minor** triad | C to Eb (minor 3rd) | C to G (perfect 5th) |
| *Example C* | an **augmented** triad | C to E (major 3rd) | C to G# (augmented 5th) |
| *Example D* | a **diminished** triad | C to Eb (minor 3rd) | C to Gb (diminished 5th) |

From this it is possible to identify the type of triad which is built on every note of the scale.

First the major scale:

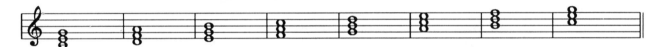

| | | | |
|---|---|---|---|
| Tonic Triad | **C to E** *Major 3rd* **C to G** *Perfect 5th* | | Major Triad |
| Supertonic Triad | **D to F** *Minor 3rd* **D to A** *Perfect 5th* | | Minor Triad |
| Mediant Triad | **E to G** *Minor 3rd* **E to B** *Perfect 5th* | | Minor Triad |
| Subdominant Triad | **F to A** *Major 3rd* **F to C** *Perfect 5th* | | Major Triad |
| Dominant Triad | **G to B** *Major 3rd* **G to D** *Perfect 5th* | | Major Triad |
| Submediant Triad | **A to C** *Minor 3rd* **A to E** *Perfect 5th* | | Minor Triad |
| Leading Note | **B to D** *Minor 3rd* **B to F** *Diminished 5th* | | Diminished Triad |

It will be seen that in a **major** scale, the tonic, subdominant and dominant triads are *major triads*, the supertonic, mediant and submediant triads are *minor triads* and the leading note triad is a *diminished triad*. The major scale does not contain an augmented triad. To use the Roman numeral system to describe these triads:

| | |
|---|---|
| Chords I, IV and V | are **major** triads |
| Chords II, III and VI | are **minor** triads |
| Chord VII | is a **diminished** triad |

When dealing with the triads belonging to the **minor** scale, there are really two versions: the harmonic and the melodic. Only the tonic triad is the same in both versions.

The triads of the **harmonic** minor scale of C minor are:

The triads of the **melodic** scale of C minor, both ascending and descending, are:

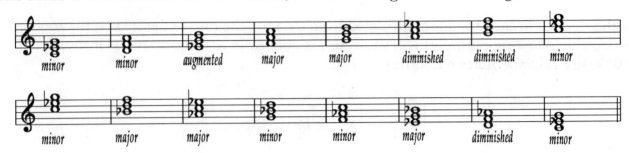

In general when harmonising chords, the harmonic minor scale and its triads are used. Wherever the leading note is written it must be sharpened. It is essential to remember this when using the chord of the dominant in the minor key: the leading note (7th degree of the scale) is the 3rd of the dominant chord and must always be sharpened, as follows:

As a triad is a chord of three notes, when more than three voices or instruments are singing or playing, one or more notes of the triad will need to be doubled. Many versions of this chord are possible, for example when written for a piano, for a string quartet, for a choir or for a full orchestra. The examples below look like six different chords, but actually they are all made from the notes of the C Major tonic triad **C, E, G**. Except for example C, the root of the chord was doubled; in example C it was the 5th of the chord which was doubled.

The chord that is being used may be worked out in exactly the same way as when dealing with triads: a chord using the notes of the tonic triad will be the tonic chord, or chord I if using Roman numerals; a chord using the notes of the dominant triad will be the dominant chord, or chord V.

Often examination questions demand that certain chords be fully described.

**Step 1**  Establish the key of the music. It is crucial to find out whether it is in a major or minor key; if this has not been clarified, the number of the chord or the degree of the scale would be incorrect, eg.

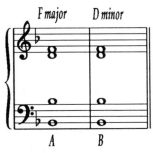

Example A          B♭ D F      F Major

subdominant chord, root position, major triad          **IVa**

Example B          B♭ D F      D Minor

submediant chord, root position, major triad          **VIa**

**Step 2**  Write down the notes of the chord. If the notes are not a third apart, eg. **C E G,** invert them until it is clear which triad is being used; it can then be seen whether the chord is in root position, 1st or 2nd inversion.

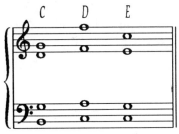

Example C          **B G D G**     1st Inversion of G B D          Chord  **Vb**
Example D          **C A F F**     2nd Inversion of F A C          Chord  **IVc**
Example E          **C G E C**     Root position of C E G          Chord  **Ia**

**Step 3**  Work out whether the chord is major, minor, augmented or diminished, in exactly the same way as in working out a triad. Give a full and complete description of the chord:

Example C          Dominant chord, 1st Inversion, Major Triad or          **Vb major triad**
Example D          Subdominant chord, 2nd Inversion, Major Triad or          **IVc major triad**
Example E          Tonic chord, Root position, Major Triad or          **Ia major triad**

# Figured Bass

**Figured Bass, Basso Continuo** (bass which 'continues through' the piece of music), or **Thorough Bass** ('through' bass) are all terms which describe a system of shorthand which composers used to enable performers to select the correct chords when supplying the accompaniment. To understand how this system evolved and when it was used it is necessary to go back to the 16th Century.

**Emilio Cavalieri** was one of the first composers to use figured bass. He was born in 1550 and spent most of his life in Florence in the employ of the Medici family. He died in Rome about 1600. Ludovico Grossi, known as **Viadana**, was born at Viadana, near Mantua, in 1564 and died in 1645. He belonged to the Franciscans, holding positions which gave him influence over ecclesiastical music, and also used figured bass extensively.

The system was in use throughout the 17th and 18th Centuries. It became prominent with the growing importance of solo recitative music, which was accompanied by plain chords. Various works in today's repertoire originally had figured bass, for example, oratorios, violin sonatas by composers such as Handel or Corelli, Bach's Brandenburg Concertos, many recitatives in operas from the time of Gluck to Mozart and much organ music.

The composer would only have written a bass line for the accompaniment, usually played on a harpsichord or organ, but would have completed his instructions by the addition of these small figures. It was an essential part of a keyboard player's skills to have a detailed and accurate knowledge of harmony and figured bass and, from this, a proficient performer could accurately construct the desired accompaniment. It also allowed him to be both inventive and artistic. The bass line was often played by cellos and double basses as well, thereby supplying a reliable foundation. The music played was expanded into the implied chords by the working out of the figures written beneath the bass note which gave the intervals of the notes to be played *above* it.

$^5_3$    *indicates*      *with the 5th*      *and the 3rd*      *played as*

These notes could be arranged in many different ways, provided that the bass note remains the same. The above example clearly illustrates that $^5_3$ means Root Position of the chord.

By the same method, it can be seen that all chords marked $^6_3$ are *first* inversions, that is, the given base with the third above and the sixth above. Again, they may be played in many arrangements.

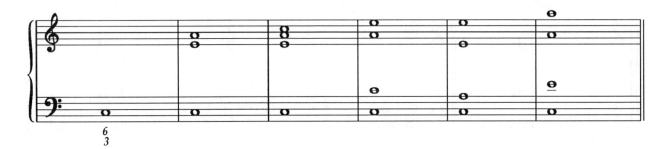

Similarly, all chords marked $^6_4$ are second inversions.

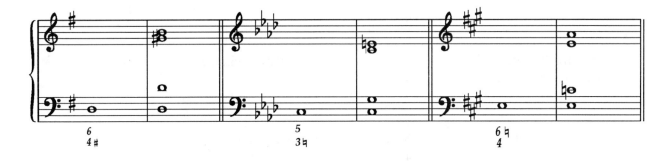

## Accidentals

An accidental placed before or after a figure applies to the note indicated by that figure:

It will be observed that an accidental added to a figured bass must be applied *even when it alters notes in the key signature.*

If a bass note has no figures, it is understood to be the root position of that note. If an accidental is used without any figures, it is applicable to the 3rd of the chord *(example A)*. Often, first inversions of chords are marked only with a 6, not the full ⁶₃ *(example B)*. If the 3rd needs to be altered, the accidental is placed under the 6 *(example C)*.

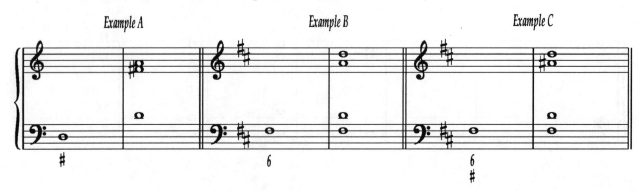

Sometimes the interval of a 7th is added to a chord to give it interest. The most commonly used chord of the 7th is that added to the dominant triad. For example, in the key of C major the dominant triad would be G B D *(example D)*, but with the 7th, it would consist of G B D and F *(example E)*. This is known as the chord of the dominant 7th.

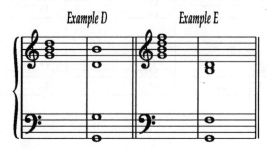

The figuring for a chord with the 7th added is:

| Root position | 7 | usually marked by | 7 |
|---|---|---|---|
| | 5 | | |
| | 3 | | |
| 1st Inversion | 6 | usually marked by | 6 |
| | 5 | | 5 |
| | 3 | | |
| 2nd Inversion | 6 | usually marked by | 4 |
| | 4 | | 3 |
| | 3 | | |
| 3rd Inversion | 6 | usually marked by | 4 |
| | 4 | | 2 |
| | 2 | | |

The added 7th gives the extra inversion, as shown below:

# Cadences

A **cadence** in speech is roughly defined as the fall of the voice at the end of a phrase or sentence. It has a similar meaning in music, being a place where the music pauses or relaxes, denoting the end of a group of words or a sentence. Logically, the point of total relaxation comes when a tune is finished, but there are other places along the way where there is a need to pause before that final stop.

Cadences do not just involve melodic notes, but chords as well. Different chords make up different cadences, but only at the end of a phrase or sentence. These same chord progressions may be used in other places, but unless they come at the end of a phrase or sentence, **they** do *not* form a cadence.

Because the tonic chord of a piece of music functions as a home base, cadences which end with the tonic chord feel as though they have come home to rest.

A **Perfect Cadence**, which gives the strongest feeling of finality, consists of chord **V** leading to chord **I**. One of the reasons for this strength is that the dominant chord contains the leading note, which 'leads' the ear to the tonic. This is particularly so when forming a perfect cadence:

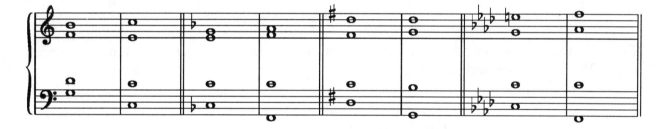

A **Plagal Cadence** (the usual progression which makes a traditional "Amen" at the end of a hymn) is chord **IV** followed by chord **I**:

Both Perfect and Plagal cadences are like full stops. However, the remaining two cadences are the equivalent of commas.

An **Imperfect Cadence** ends on chord **V**, the dominant, and gives the effect of a short pause, as does a comma. One of several chords may be used *before* chord **V**, for example chords **I**, **II**, **IV** or **VI**. The following are imperfect cadences using these different chords; for ease of recognition they are all imperfect cadences in the key of C major.

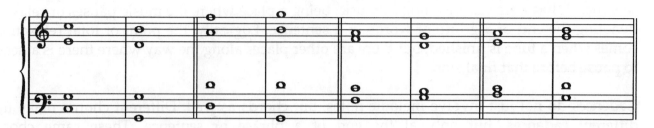

An **Interrupted Cadence** ends on chord **VI** and is something of an aural surprise. It really does sound interrupted or unfinished. It may be preceded by any chord except the tonic, but the most commonly used progression is *dominant* to *sub-mediant*, chords **V** to **VI**.

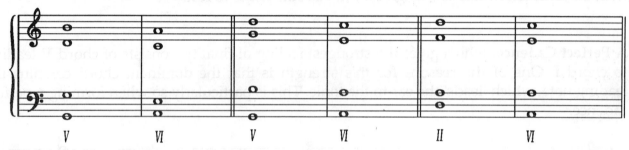

Normally the second chord of the cadence will come on a stronger beat than the preceding chord. Where the second chord is the weaker accent of the two chords, this is termed a **feminine ending**.

# Choral Writing

In choral music the voices are usually divided into four groups: **soprano** (high female), **alto** (low female), **tenor** (high male) and **bass** (low male). A choir is usually made up of Soprano, Alto, Tenor and Bass sections, often abbreviated to **S. A. T. B**. Choral singers in Church music are termed a **Choir** and in opera or other staged music, a **Chorus**.

There are two ways of notating music for choirs: **Open Score**, where each part has a line to itself; and **Short Score**, where the male voices share one stave in the bass clef and the female voices the other stave in the treble clef. Below are the first four bars of a well-known hymn tune written first in open score, then in short score:

**Open Score**

**Short score:**

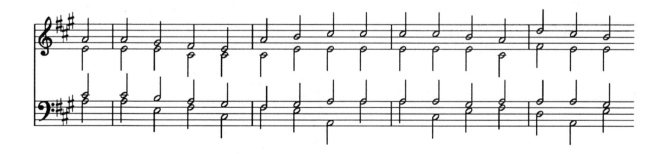

Although these two versions look very different on paper, they sound identical.

It should be understood that voices vary, some having larger or smaller ranges, but the usual compass of notes which each group can be expected to sing is as follows:

|  Soprano | Alto | Tenor | Bass |

There are a few simple rules which explain the difference between open and short score.

# Open Score

1       Each part has its own stave
2       The stems of the notes conform to normal practice, ie. if the note is on the middle line the stem may go up or down; if it is above the middle line, the stem goes down; if it is below the middle line, the stem goes up.
3       Each stave has a separate bar-line.
4       The tenor part is actually written an octave higher than it is sung. In practice this never presents a difficulty: tenors automatically sing the part in their masculine range. Modern printing practice sometimes inserts a small **8** under the Treble Clef of the tenor part to indicate that it will sound an octave lower.

# Short Score

1       Soprano and alto share the treble clef stave; tenor and bass share the bass clef stave.
2       The soprano and tenor stems will always point upwards, even if pitched *below* the alto and bass parts.
        The alto and bass stems will always point downwards, even if pitched *above* the soprano and tenor parts.
        This makes the individual parts immediately visible, eg.

| 3 | Each stave has a separate bar line. |
|---|---|
| 4 | The tenor part uses the bass clef and is written at its proper pitch. |
| 5 | Although accidentals last for a bar, this only applies to the *part* to which it has been given. If it needs to be used by the other part on that stave within the bar, unlike piano music it must be re-written. |

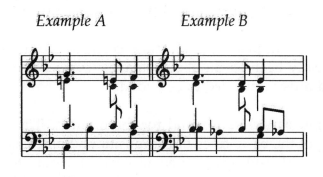

*Example A*          *Example B*

In example **A** the alto part just had **E natural**; the natural sign needed to be re-written for the sopranos.

In example **B** the basses first had **A flat**; the flat sign needed to be re-written for the tenors.

# Writing a Melody

This exercise gives scope for the learning of the basic rules of composition. It is really a continuation of the earlier exercise of composing a reply to a given phrase, but now the student is given the freedom and responsibility to produce the original musical idea.

Music is so much more than just writing a tune consisting of notes and bars of the correct length. Much has already been learnt about balance, correct stress and the use of material. Now imagination and musicality need to be added.

Many tunes are of eight bars duration and for the moment it is of sufficient length to give scope for the learning of the basic rules of composition. (Some examinations actually specify this length.) The melody should be complete in itself. It should feel and sound finished, not as though it had been left in mid-air. Try to develop the ability to *hear* what is written without playing it on an instrument.

In any melody the important elements are *rhythm* and *pitch*. Right at the beginning try to decide whether the composition is to be fast or slow. Next, decide on the time-signature. At this point, tap two or three bars at the chosen speed and time signature.

You might have, for example:

**Adagio** $^3_4$      Tap   ♩ ♩ ♩ | ♩ ♩ ♩ | ♩ ♩ ♩ | ♩. ‖

This gives one phrase length at the selected slow tempo and even at this early stage a rhythm might be taking shape. For example:

**Adagio** $^3_4$        ♩ ♩ ♩ | ♩ ♩ | ♩ ♩. ♪♩ | ♩. ‖

As a shape to the phrase emerges, some sounds may suggest themselves. At this point, the pitch of the notes to be used needs consideration. The instrument for which the composition is intended will impose certain limitations of pitch: a violin or flute, for example, will play higher notes than a cello or bassoon.

Decide whether the tune will be in a major or minor key. This decision will influence the colour and consequently the mood of the composition.

Think about the character of the composition. If it is to be cheerful, even chirpy, staccato notes and rests might be included and it certainly would not have a very slow tempo. If it is to be very sad, longer value notes and rests would be needed together with a more legato approach.

Is the melody to be loud or soft, or to change from loud to soft, or soft to loud? If so, appropriate expression marks are needed. Is the tempo to remain constant throughout, or is it to change? If so, rallentando or accelerando, or any other instructions of tempo must be written in.

Every one of these decisions has to be annotated, and particular care is needed when writing slurs. Make it absolutely clear where they begin and where they finish. When only one instrument is playing, the slur should be placed near the head of the notes (*example a*) and not near the tail (*example b*):

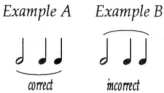

If there are stems in both directions, place the slur *above* the notes.

When a phrase mark is also present, slurs, ties and staccato dots *must* be placed *inside*, not outside, the phrase mark.

It might help at this point to take a well-known hymn-tune and analyse how it is written. This tune of eight bars is perfectly balanced, has variety and is interesting.

There are four phrases of two bars. Each phrase is satisfactory, or *satisfying*, in itself. Bars 3 and 4 reply to bars 1 and 2; bars 7 and 8 reply to bars 5 and 6. Bars 5, 6, 7 and 8 answer fully bars 1, 2, 3 and 4.

Bar 3 has the same rhythm as bar 1; bars 6 and 8 have the same rhythm as bar 4; bar 7 has the same rhythm as bar 5. The one surprise is in bar 2, but this musical jolt is only done once to give the tune life by running up the scale.

Consider how the composer has organised the pitch of the notes. He begins on the lower tonic and finishes on the higher tonic. At the half-way point he has gone to the dominant, which is what many composers do. It is worth remembering that whilst this composer has used the root of the chords of the tonic and dominant, another composer might have selected a different note from those chords, either the 3rd or the 5th. The effect would be perfectly in order.

Bar 1 uses only notes from the tonic chord, starting low. Bar 2 is part of an *ascending* scale. Bar 3 goes yet higher in order to come down the scale to the dominant in bar 4. Bar 5 shoots up again. Bar 7 is the climax of the tune and has a similar rhythm to that of bar 5. Bar 8 rounds off the tune, ending on the higher tonic.

Below are some examples of similar pitch organisation, but using $^3_4$ time, and in C minor, not C major:

*Version 1:*

*Version 2:*

*Version 3:*

Note how bar 6 in version 3 used bar 2 in contrary motion.

When working in the minor key, care must be taken in approaching and leaving the leading note. In good melodic writing - especially in singing - the interval of an augmented second is awkward and unmelodic. In a minor scale, when the leading note is sharpened, an augmented second is immediately produced. It follows that in melody writing a much better result is obtained by using the melodic minor scale, not the harmonic. Therefore the 6th and 7th notes are sharpened when ascending, and those accidentals are cancelled when descending. Although in bar 2, which is *ascending*, the descending version has been used, this is perfectly in order because it is melodious and pleasing to the ear. (Refer to pages 27-9.)

Obviously not all tunes are eight bars in length. Consider the following versions of 5, 6 and 7 bars' length, then compare them with the 8-bar versions above. If it *feels* right, then it stands a good chance of being musically acceptable; but in spite of the unusual phrase length it *must* still feel balanced.

It will be seen from this that the number of ways in which even this small amount of material can be arranged are many. This is one of the fascinations of music. It is like watching the sea: to one person all waves are just waves; to the discerning watcher, each wave is different.

# Writing a Song

The basis of writing a song is a combination of the guidelines set out in the previous section and in the earlier one on **How to write a rhythm to words**. These rules need to be applied in order to accommodate the words in a musical fashion.

Using the same words, in order to given continuity to the process, repeat steps 1 to 7 beginning on page 49 in order to obtain a suitable rhythm and a time signature. Example F on page 51 will be used to illustrate the rest of this section.

The following need to be considered in order to produce a musical tune:

1. Balance
2. Sense of completion
3. Unifying the whole by the usage of the given material
4. Imagination
5. Musicality
6. Tempo
7. Expression marks
8. Mood
9. Key
10. Major or Minor scale
11. The type of voice for whom the song is intended. Remember that no singer will want to repeat the highest or lowest notes frequently. Use the extremes of pitch for special effects; there are plenty of other notes in between!

All these points need to be thought about *before* beginning the composition.

**Points 1 to 5** cannot really be decided beforehand and will be dealt with in the working of the exercise.

**Point 6** - For the purpose of this exercise a moderate tempo is chosen, so the instruction might be *moderato, andante* or perhaps *allegretto*.

**Point 7** - This will be dealt with later.

**Point 8** - These particular words suggest a happy mood.

**Points 9 & 10** - The scale of F major.

**Point 11** - A tenor voice. When writing for the tenor voice, it is usual to use the treble clef unless writing four-part harmony in short score. (See page 82.)

A number of things can now be filled in:

    **1**   Tempo instruction - **andante**

    **2**   Key signature - **F major**

    **3**   Time signature - $\frac{4}{4}$

    **4**   The words, which must be written out in separate syllables, need plenty of space between them. It is a good idea to pencil in the total time value allocated to each syllable. More than one note might be given to a syllable and this will show what the *total* value should be.

    **5**   Insert the bar lines. This will give a visible framework to the composition. Note two points:

a) When a tune does not begin on the first beat of the bar, the first and last notes must total a full bar. Because of the natural accents of the words, this tune begins on the fourth beat.

b) For the same reason, the last syllable of the first line, *'cloud'*, and the first syllable of the second line, *'that'*, are in the same bar. When performance directions are added the phrase mark will make it visually clear where the first line ends and the second begins.

The skeleton of the composition should now be apparent and actually leads to the composition of the tune.

Refer back to the previous chapter and consider whether the use of landmarks such as lower tonic, dominant and upper tonic might help, especially on strong syllables. The next stage might look something like this:

Quite often when setting words to music, the words themselves dictate or suggest things and it is useful to be receptive to these suggestions. The result will seem more natural and *feel* more satisfactory.

**Two points:**

**1  Technical**    When the song does not start on the first beat of the bar because of word-stress, it has to be considered which notes are going to be used, and consequently which chords they imply. The two are inextricably bound, at least to Western ears. A common opening might be one where the first strong syllable belongs to the tonic chord; therefore the preceding note or notes might belong to the dominant. That is the progression implied here. It could just as well be the other way round: when starting on the tonic  the dominant would be allocated to the syllable *wan-*.

**2  Imaginative**    Words automatically suggest pictures and colours. When speaking these are implied, usually unconsciously, by the pitch of the speaking voice. In music much more precision and awareness are necessary. Words like *cloud, float, high* and *hill* all suggest height: consider using higher-pitched notes on them. Decide which syllable might have the highest note; perhaps in this case it should come on the syllable *high*. Words like *lonely* and *vale* suggest a lower pitch. Remember that most notes can be altered; have the courage to experiment. Refer to the eight different versions for one exercise on page 55.

Try to begin to plot a few more landmarks. Keeping the general directions in mind, and also remembering the range of the voice, the next stage might be:

The gaps now need to be filled in:

This melody is rather like a room with furniture, but without carpets, curtains or pictures: adequate, but without comfort. On page 51, it was suggested that some syllables would need more than one note to help to illustrate the word sense. So perhaps the next stage might be something like this:

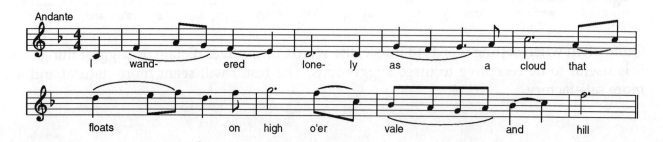

**Page 90**

Lastly, the performance directions need to be inserted. The following might be one possible result:

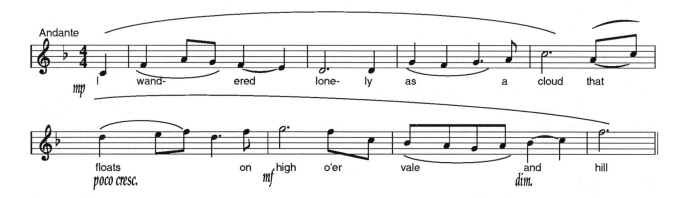

This tune has been composed by a fairly systematic method, but it is not the only way of composing. When Beethoven composed his Fifth Symphony, it is possible that the first few notes came to him as a revelation or inspiration, or alternatively as a result of much prior thought. Listen to the symphony and remind yourself how much he made out of these four notes:

If a tune begins to suggest itself, write it down and explore what you can do with it.

# Binary and Ternary Form

Pages 52 to 55 showed how a tune of eight bars could be constructed so that it became a balanced and interesting musical sentence. Most musical compositions need to be far longer than eight bars; this can be achieved by using such a sentence economically and inventively.

In the same way that a recipe gives guidelines for cooking, so guidelines are needed in structuring music. The two most basic musical structures or forms are known as **Binary** and **Ternary**. *Binary* means to do with *two*; *Ternary* means to do with *three*.

### Binary Form

This was the overall pattern of simple musical movements until the middle of the eighteenth century. Bach used it extensively in his dance suites in such movements as minuets and gavottes. It indicates that the piece is roughly divided into two halves. The first half is the opening statement, which usually modulates to the key of the dominant. (**Modulation** is the musical journey from one key to another.) The second half continues in the key which has just been reached, and then leads back to the tonic. Material from the first half - for example, rhythmic patterns - may be used in the second half.

In the following example, material from the third version of the eight-bar musical sentence on page 86 has been used. (This is shown first, for ease of comparison.)

**Original:**   1          2          3    4          5              6          7          8

**New version in Binary form:**

Many ideas from the original eight bars have been incorporated into this; however the most important consideration is that the dominant key has been established at the half-way mark by a perfect cadence in G minor in bars 7 and 8. Bar 9 begins the second half in G minor, but by bar 11 the tune has returned to the home key of C minor.

To show how the material has been used, here follows a bar by bar analysis:

| | |
|---|---|
| *Bar 1* | same as original |
| *Bar 2* | same as original |
| *Bar 3* | original version transposed down a fifth |
| *Bar 4* | bar 6 in original version, but one octave lower |
| *Bar 5* | new material |
| *Bar 6* | original bar 6 in contrary motion, but in new key of G minor |
| *Bar 7* | original bar 6 in G minor, with last note adjusted to make perfect cadence |
| *Bar 8* | same as bar 4 |
| *Bar 9* | similar idea to bar 1 |
| *Bar 10* | sequence of bar 5 in the original version |
| *Bar 11* | similar idea to bar 1 |
| *Bar 12* | same as bar 6 in the original version |
| *Bar 13* | sequence of bar 12 |
| *Bar 14* | bar 1 in contrary motion |
| *Bar 15* | same as bar 5 in the original version |
| *Bar 16* | same as bar 8 in the original version |

**Ternary Form**

The development of Ternary Form began during the lifetime of Handel. Although both he and Bach were born in 1685, their work developed in very different ways.

Ternary means a tune that has *three* main parts:
*Part 1* - A musical sentence which does not necessarily have to modulate.
*Part 2* - A completely different, but *always balancing*, musical statement.
*Part 3* - The opening statement repeated.

As this pattern became established, part one was repeated, but not part three. Many of Mozart's minuets were in ternary form, and this developed - when extended - into the pattern of the third movement of the classical symphony.

In this example, the opening sentence has been derived from the original version on the previous page. Repeat marks are included, and often there would be a different expression mark for the repeat. Bars 9 to 16 are new, and bars 17 to 24 repeat the original sentence.

# Appendix 1a - Remaining tonic triads in major keys

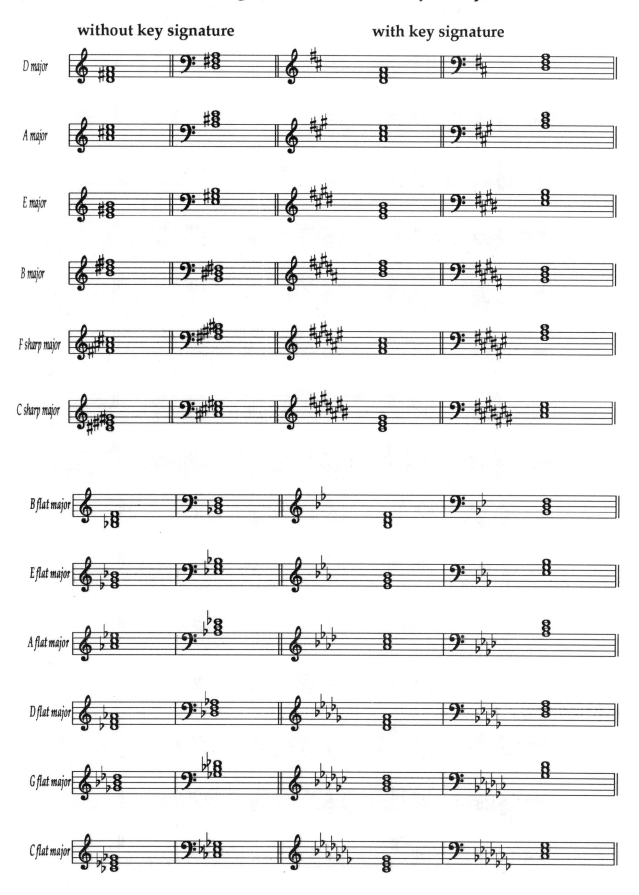

# Appendix 1b - Remaining tonic triads in minor keys

### without key signature

### with key signature

# Appendix 2a - Italian Terms

| | |
|---|---|
| *a* | at, to, for, in the style of |
| *a cappella* | without accompaniment (lit. in church style) |
| *accelerando, accel.* | gradually getting faster |
| *adagietto* | a little faster than *adagio* |
| *adagio* | slow, leisurely |
| *a due, a2* | for two players or singers (sometimes meaning they are to play in unison) |
| *ad libitum, ad lib* | freely, at pleasure |
| *affetuoso* | tenderly |
| *affretando, affret* | hurrying |
| *agitato* | agitated |
| *alla, al* | in the manner of |
| *alla breve* | with a minim beat (The music usually sounds faster than the printed notes suggest.) |
| *alla marcia* | like a march |
| *allargando* | becoming a little slower and louder |
| *allegro* | fast |
| *alt* | high |
| *amabile* | pleasant |
| *amore* | love |
| *amoroso* | loving |
| *anima* | soul |
| *con anima* | with feeling or with spirit |
| *animando* | becoming more lively |
| *animato* | animated |
| *a piacere* | at pleasure, freely |
| *appassionato* | with passion |
| *arco* | with the bow |
| *assai* | very |
| *a tempo* | in time (Usually used after slowing down.) |
| *attaca* | go straight on |
| *bene, ben* | very; well |
| *bis* | twice (Usually applied to a bar or short passage.) |
| *bravura* | brilliance |
| *con bravura* | with brilliance |
| *brillante* | brilliant |
| *brio* | vigour |
| *brioso, con brio* | with vigour |
| *calando* | dying away in tone and speed |
| *calmato* | tranquil |
| *cantabile* | in a singing style |
| *cantando* | singing |
| *capriccioso* | whimsical, fanciful |
| *coll, colla, colle* | with, with the |
| *colla parte* | with the solo part |
| *colla voce* | with the voice |
| *col legno* | with the wood (ie. string players are to use the wooden part of the bow) |
| *coll' ottava* | add the notes of the higher or lower octave in keyboard music |
| *come* | as |
| *come prima* | as previously |
| *come sopra* | as above (similar to *come prima*) |
| *comodo* | convenient |
| *con* | with |
| *corda, corde* | strings |
| *crescendo, cresc, cres* | gradually getting louder |
| *da* | from |
| *da capo, D.C.* | repeat from the beginning |
| *dal segno, D.S.* | repeat from the sign |
| *deciso* | firmly |
| *decrescendo, decresc, decres* | gradually getting quieter |
| *delicato* | delicately |
| *diminuendo, dim* | gradually getting quieter |
| *divisi, div* | orchestral players are to divide into two or more groups |
| *dolente* | sad, mournful |
| *dolore* | grief |
| *doloroso* | sorrowful |
| *doppio movimento* | twice as fast |
| *e, ed* | and |
| *energico* | energetic |
| *espressione* | expression |
| *espressivo* | expressive |
| *estinto* | very quietly, lifeless |
| *facile* | easy |
| *felice* | happy |
| *feroce* | fierce |
| *fine* | end |
| *flessibile* | not in strict time |
| *forza* | force |
| *fretta* | haste |
| *fuoco* | fire |
| *furioso* | furious |
| *giocoso* | playful |
| *giojoso* | joyful |
| *giusto* | exact |
| G.P. (General Pause) | all performers are to be silent |
| *grandioso* | grandly |
| *grazioso* | graceful |
| *impetuoso* | impetuous |
| *in alt* | In vocal music this refers to the notes in the octave above the treble clef. |

| | | | |
|---|---|---|---|
| incalzando | pressing forward | pochissimo | very little |
| | | poco | little |
| lacrimoso | sad, tearful | poco a poco | little by little, gradually |
| lamentoso | lamenting | poi | then |
| liberamente | freely | ponticello | bridge |
| licenza | licence, freedom | sul ponticello | near (literally on) the bridge |
| l'istesso | the same | portamento | carrying, sliding from one note to the next |
| l'istesso tempo | at the same pace | | |
| loco | at the normal pitch (Used to cancel an *8va* instruction.) | possibile | possible |
| | | precipitando, precipitoso | rushing, impetuously |
| lontano | distant | prima, primo | first |
| lugubre | mournful | | |
| lusingando | coaxing, persuasively | quasi | as if, like |
| | | | |
| ma | but | repetizione | repetition |
| maestoso | majestically | rigoroso | strict |
| mano | hand | rinforzando | reinforcing |
| mano destra | right hand | risoluto | strong, bold |
| mano sinistra | left hand | ritmico | rhythmically |
| mancando | fading away | rubato | literally 'robbed' |
| marcato | marked | tempo rubato | with some freedom of time |
| martellato | hammered | | |
| marziale | like a march | scherzando, scherzoso | joking, playful |
| meno | less | secco | dry |
| mesto | sad | seconda, secondo | second |
| mezza, mezzo | half | segue | straight on |
| mezza voce | half voice, in an undertone | semplice | simple |
| misterioso | mysterious | sempre | always |
| misura | measure | senza | without |
| molto | much | sforzando, sfz, sf | forced, accented |
| morendo | dying away | simile | in the same way |
| mosso | with motion or movement | slargando | getting slower |
| moto, movimento | movement, motion | slancio | enthusiasm |
| | | slentando | getting slower |
| niente | nothing | smorzando | losing both tone and speed |
| nobilmente | nobly | soave | gentle |
| non | not | solenne | solemn |
| nuovo | new | sonoramente | with a rich tone |
| | | sopra | above |
| obbligato | obligatory | sordino | mute |
| ossio | or | sordini | mutes |
| ottava | octave | sospirando | sighing |
| | | sostenuto | sustained |
| parlando | speaking | sotto | below |
| pausa | pause | sotto voce | in an undertone |
| pedale | pedal | spiccato | bouncing (Usually a term for string players.) |
| per | by | | |
| perpendosi | dying away | spiritoso | spirited |
| pesante | heavily | staccato | detached, short |
| piacevole | pleasant | strepitoso | boisterous |
| piangevole | plaintive, like a lament | stretto | 1: quickening the speed; 2: where the entries in a fugue overlap |
| pietoso | pitifully | | |
| piu | more | | |
| pizzicato, pizz | plucked | stringendo | getting faster |
| placido | calm | subito | suddenly |
| pochettino | rather little | sul, sulla | on the |

| | | | |
|---|---|---|---|
| *tacet* | silent | *feurig* | fiery |
| *tanto* | so much | *Flatterzunge, Flzg* | fluttering-tonguing (applied to wind instruments) |
| *tasto* | the fingerboard of a string instrument | *fliessend* | flowing |
| *tempo* | speed, pace | *frei* | free |
| *teneramente* | tenderly | *frisch* | vigorous, fresh, bright |
| *tenuto* | held | *fröhlich* | joyful, cheerful |
| *tosto* | swift | | |
| *tranquillo* | calm | *gebunden* | joined |
| *tre* | three | *gehend* | steadily (= *andante*) |
| *tremolando, tremole* | trembling | *gesangvoll* | in a singing style (= *cantabile*) |
| *trionfale* | triumphant | *geschwind* | quick |
| *tristamente* | sad | | |
| *troppo* | too much | *immer* | always |
| *tutti* | all | *innig* | sincere, heartfelt |
| | | | |
| *una, uno* | one | *kräftig* | strong |
| *unisono, unis* | in unison | | |
| | | *langsam* | slow (= *lento*) |
| *veloce* | swift | *lebhaft* | lively |
| *vibrato* | vibrating | *leicht* | light |
| *vigoroso* | vigorous | *Leid* | pain, grief |
| *vivace, vivo* | lively | *leidvoll, leidensvoll* | sorrowful |
| *voce* | voice | *Leidenschaft* | passion |
| *volante* | flying | *leidenschaftlich* | passionate |
| *volta* | time | *leise* | gentle, soft |
| *seconda volta* | second time | *lieblich* | lovely |
| *volti subito, V.S.* | Turn the page immediately. | *lustig* | cheerful |
| | | | |
| | | *mässig* | at a moderate speed |
| | | *mit* | with |
| | | *munter* | lively |
| | | | |
| | | *nach und nach* | gradually |
| | | *nicht* | not |
| | | *noch* | yet, still |

## Appendix 2b - German Terms

| | | | |
|---|---|---|---|
| | | *ohne* | without |
| *aber* | but | *rasch* | quick |
| *als* | than | *rascher* | quicker |
| *Ausdruck* | expression | *ruhig* | peaceful |
| *ausdrucksvoll* | expressively | | |
| | | *schnell* | fast |
| *bestimmt* | with decision, definite | *schneller* | faster |
| *bewegt* | with movement, agitated | *schwach* | weak |
| *breit* | broad, expansive | *schwächer* | weaker |
| | | *sehr* | very |
| *Dämpfer* | mute | *stark* | strong |
| *doch* | however | *süss* | sweet |
| | | | |
| *ein* | a | *traurig* | sad |
| *einfach* | simple | | |
| *Empfindung* | feeling, emotion | *und* | and |
| *empfindungsvoll* | with feeling | | |
| *etwas* | rather, somewhat | | |

| | | | | |
|---|---|---|---|---|
| *viel* | much | | *gracieux* | graceful |
| *voll* | full | | *grave* | very slow and solemn |
| *vorgetragen* | prominent | | | |
| | | | *joyeux* | joyful |
| *wenig* | little | | | |
| *wieder* | again | | *légèrement* | lightly |
| | | | *lent* | slow |
| *zart* | tender | | *librement* | freely |
| *ziemlich* | moderately | | *lointain* | distant |
| *zu* | too, to | | *lourd* | heavy |

| | |
|---|---|
| *main* | hand |
| *main gauche* | left hand |
| *main droite* | right hand |
| *mais* | but |
| *martelé* | hammered |
| *moins* | less |
| *mouvement* | movement |

## Appendix 2c - French Terms

| | |
|---|---|
| *non* | not |

| | | | | |
|---|---|---|---|---|
| *à deux, à2* | two instruments or performers (Occasionally, as in orchestral music, it indicates that a part is to be performed in unision by two players.) | | *pédale* | pedal |
| | | | *peu* | little |
| | | | *peu a peu* | little by little |
| | | | *plus* | more |
| | | | *presser, pressez* | hurry |
| *amour* | love | | | |
| *apaisé* | calmed | | *ralentir* | slow down |
| *assez* | very | | *retunu* | held back |
| *avec* | with | | | |
| | | | *sans* | without |
| *cédez* | yield; a slightly more relaxed tempo | | *sec* | crisp, dry |
| | | | *seul* | alone |
| *comme* | as | | *serrer, serrez* | gradually getting faster |
| | | | | |
| *détaché* | detached | | *sonore* | resonant |
| *douce, doux* | soft, sweet | | *sourdine* | mute |
| *doucement* | softly, sweetly | | *sous* | under |
| | | | | |
| *égal* | equal | | *très* | very |
| *emporté* | fiery | | *triste* | sad |
| *en animent* | becoming more lively | | | |
| *en cédant* | yielding | | *un, une* | one |
| *en dehors* | prominent | | | |
| *enlevez* | take off (as applied to a pedal or mute) | | *vif* | lively, animated, brisk |
| | | | *vite* | quickly |
| *en mesure* | in time | | *vivement* | lively |
| *en pressant* | hurrying | | | |
| *en retenant* | slowing the tempo a little | | | |
| *en serrant* | becoming quicker | | | |
| *expressif* | expressively | | | |
| *et* | and | | | |
| | | | | |
| *facile* | easy | | | |
| *fin* | end | | | |
| *flottant* | floating | | | |

# Index

## A
accent     7
acciaccatura     64, 70
accidentals     19, 60-61, 77-78
accuracy     12
alto clef     48
appoggiatura     63-64

## B
balance     12, 52-53, 88
bar     7
bar-line     7, 50
bass clef     2-4
basso continuo     76
beat     5, 7, 9, 12, 50, 62
Binary Form     92
breve     5

## C
C clef     48
cadence     79-80
chord     71, 75-78
chromatic scale     46
clef     1
common time     8
compound intervals     38
Compound Time     7, 22-24
concord     39

## D
diatomic scales     14
discord     39
dissonance     64
dominant     30
dotted notes     6
duple time     24
duplet     24

## F
Figured Bass     76
flat     18-19

## G
grace notes     70

## H
harmonic minor     25-26, 40-41, 74
harmony     71-72

## I
imagination     12, 51, 88
imperfect cadence     80
interrupted cadence     80
interval     27, 35-37, 73
inversion     72

## K
key     56, 58, 75
key signature     19-20

## L
leading note     30
ledger lines     4, 48

## M
major     14
major scale     15
mediant     30
melodic minor     27-29, 42-43
melody     71
Middle C     1-2, 4, 73
minor     14
mode     14
modulation     92
mordent     64-66
musical sentence     52

## N
natural     19
note     5

## O
octave     2
Open Score     81-82
ornament     63

## P
perfect cadence     79
phrase mark     6
pitch     1-2, 54, 84
plagal cadence     79

**Q**

quadruple time      24

**R**

rest      5, 10, 62
rhythm      12, 49, 54, 62, 84

**S**

scale      14
semibreve      5
semitone      14-15, 46-47
sharp      16, 19
Short score      81-82
Simple Time      7-8, 24
slur      6, 85
split time      8
staff      1
stave      1
stress      62
sub-dominant      30
sub-mediant      30
supertonic      30
syncopation      62

**T**

tenor clef      48
Ternary Form      93
tetrachord      16-18
Thorough Bass      76
tie      6
Tied notes      6
time signature      8, 22, 50
tone      14-15
tonic      30
tonic triad      21
transposition      56
treble clef      2-4
triad      21, 74
trill      69-70
triple time      24
triplet      11
tritone      39
turn      66-68, 70